国家出版基金项目
NATIONAL PUBLICATION FOUNDATION

CHINESE RED
中国红

中国建筑装饰

Chinese Architectural Decoration

金夏◎编著

全国百佳图书出版单位
APTIME 时代出版传媒股份有限公司
时代出版 黄 山 书 社

图书在版编目(CIP)数据

中国建筑装饰：汉英对照／金夏编著. ——合肥：黄山书社, 2012.8

（中国红）

ISBN 978-7-5461-3081-1

Ⅰ.①中… Ⅱ.①金… Ⅲ.①古建筑－建筑装饰－中国 Ⅳ.①TU-092.2

中国版本图书馆CIP数据核字(2012)第198811号

中国建筑装饰
ZHONG GUO JIAN ZHU ZHUANG SHI   金 夏 编著

出 版 人：任耕耘

责任编辑：司 雯 李 南   特约编辑：朱昌爱
责任印制：戚 帅 李 磊   装帧设计：商子庄

出版发行：时代出版传媒股份有限公司（http://www.press-mart.com）
　　　　　黄山书社（http://www.hsbook.cn）
　　　　　（合肥市蜀山区翡翠路1118号出版传媒广场7层　邮编：230071）
经　　销：新华书店　　　　　　　营销电话：0551-3533762　3533768
印　　刷：合肥精艺印刷有限公司　　电　　话：0551-4859368

开　　本：710×875　1/16　　　　印张：12　　　　字数：153千字
版　　次：2012年8月第1版　　　2012年8月第1次印刷
书　　号：ISBN 978-7-5461-3081-1　　　定价：59.00元

建筑是人类基本的实践活动之一，是人类文明的产物。在世界上，以宫廷木结构建筑为代表的中国传统建筑、以比萨斜塔为代表的意大利罗马建筑，和以巴黎圣母院为代表的法国哥特式建筑，并称为三大传统建筑体系，在全球范围内有着广泛的影响。中国传统建筑装饰是中国传统建筑必不可少的组成部分。这些装饰本身既有一定的实用价值，又有很强的艺术感染力，表现了强烈的民族风格和时代特征。

随着建筑材料和技术的改进，中国传统建筑装饰出现了很多不同的变化，而这些变化又与各个历史时期的政治、经

Building is one of the basic activities of human beings and a product of human civilization. Chinese traditional architecture represented by the royal wood frame buildings, Roman architecture represented by the Leaning Tower of Pisa and French Gothic architecture represented by Notre Dame de Paris are known as the three traditional building systems that have had an extensive impact throughout the world. The traditional Chinese architectural decoration is an essential part of traditional Chinese buildings. The decoration itself has some practical value and a strong artistic appeal, showing a strong national style and characteristics of the times.

With the improvement of building materials and technology, traditional Chinese architectural decoration has changed a lot. The change is closely related to political, economic, cultural, aesthetic and other ideological factors at various historical

济、文化、审美等意识形态密切相关。根据建筑的形态、部位、等级及材料的不同，建筑装饰的形式也有所不同。本书通过对中国传统建筑装饰的历史、种类、特点及工艺材料、装饰构件等内容的梳理，系统、全面地向读者展现中国传统建筑装饰文化。希望通过本书的内容，读者能够更多地了解中国传统建筑装饰的魅力。

periods. Forms of architectural decoration differ according to different building shapes, locations, grades and materials. This book analyzes elements such as the history, kinds, features, craft materials and decorative elements of traditional Chinese architectural decoration to demonstrate to readers its culture in a systematic and comprehensive way. Hopefully readers can learn more about the charm of traditional Chinese architectural decoration through reading this book.

目 录 Contents

源远流长的历史
Time-honored History

　　中国传统建筑是指从先秦（前21世纪—前221）到19世纪中叶以前的建筑，是一个独立形成的建筑体系。和世界其他民族一样，中国古代的先民也经历了自穴居、巢居，到地面上建造房屋的过程，并形成了以木结构为主的建筑方式。这种建筑方式成为世界上延续时间最长、分布地域最广、风格极其鲜明的建筑体系。建筑的装饰是伴随着建筑的出现而产生的，中国古代劳动人民的智慧结晶创造出了各式各样的建筑样式，也随之出现了种类繁多、五彩缤纷的建筑装饰。而且这些建筑装饰还起到了调整建筑构造、比例的作用，其保护建筑本身、延长建筑寿命的功用也不可忽略。

Traditional Chinese architecture refers to the building system independently-formed from the pre-Qin period (21st century B.C.–221 B.C.) to the mid-19th century. Like other peoples of the world, the ancient Chinese also went through the process of living in caves, on trees, and finally building houses on the ground and forming a building style featuring mainly wooden structures that became the most widely distributed building system with a very distinctive style which lasts the longest in the world. Architectural decoration comes into being along with the emergence of architecture. The working people of ancient China created a wide variety of architectural styles with their skill and knowledge, resulting in a wide range of colorful architectural decoration. The architectural decoration also played a role in adjusting the structure and proportion of the buildings. Its role in protecting the building itself and extending its service life can also not be ignored.

> 传统建筑装饰的发展

在中国古代文字甲骨文中，有不少关于建筑的文字，根据这些字形推测，公元前1000多年前的商朝，人们居住的房屋有的是建在台基之上，有的是干栏式住宅，虽然墙体很少装饰，但部分房屋的屋脊已经开始使用高耸的装饰构件。

大约在西周（前1046—前771）初期，除了覆盖屋顶用的板瓦和半

• 半瓦当
Semi-Circle Eaves Tile

> Development of Traditional Architectural Decoration

The ancient Chinese oracle bone inscriptions have a lot of characters related to buildings. Based on these fonts, it can be presumed that in the Shang Dynasty (1600 B.C.-1046 B.C.), some of the houses that people lived in were built on top of a podium, and some were built to be stilt houses. Although there was little decoration on the wall, tall decorative components were already used on the ridges of some houses.

In the early period of the Western Zhou Dynasty (1046 B.C.-771 B.C.), in addition to the roof-covering plain tiles and the semi-cylindrical tiles, there emerged simple pattern tiles to decorate the cornice and protect the eaves.

In the Spring and Autumn Period (770 B.C.-476 B.C.), people began

• 鹿纹瓦当
Deer Pattern Eaves Tile

圆筒形的筒瓦之外，还出现了用于装饰檐口、保护屋檐的半圆形的素纹瓦当。

春秋时期（前770—前476），人们开始重视对居室内的装饰，出现了木建筑彩画。大约在春秋至战国（前475—前221）时期，开始出现圆形瓦当，这些瓦当有了很强的装饰性，有各种精美的纹样，如夔龙纹、夔凤纹、鹿纹等。

从东汉（25—220）到三国时期（220—280）的建筑，开始重视利用屋顶的形式和瓦进行装饰。屋顶形式以悬山式和庑殿式最为常见。门上多装饰有门簪，门扇多装

to focus on interior decoration and decorative color paintings for wooden buildings appeared. Round eaves tiles began to appear in around the Spring and Autumn Period to the Warring States Period (475 B.C.-221 B.C.). They were highly decorative and have various exquisite patterns, such as *Kui* dragon, *Kui* phoenix and deer.

From the Eastern Han Dynasty (25-220) to the Three Kingdoms Period (220-280), people began to pay attention to the usage of roof forms and tiles for decoration. The commonly-seen roof forms are overhanging gable roof and hipped roof. Doors were often decorated with cylinders and door leaves were often decorated with door knockers. Mullioned windows were often used and sometimes other patterns were decorated on the windows. Animal prints were seen as decoration on some roof ridges.

During the Wei, Jin, Southern and Northern Dynasties (220-589), as Buddhism and Taoism had more influence in the private sector, relevant decorative patterns began to be applied to architectural decoration, such as the lotus and the Eight Diagrams patterns. Royal families often had hipped roofs. The roof ridge was often decorated with an owl-

饰以辅首。建筑上的窗常见的是直棂窗，也有的在窗上装饰其他花纹。有的屋脊开始使用动物图案进行装饰。

魏晋南北朝（220—589）时期，随着佛教、道教在民间的影响逐渐加大，一些与之相关的装饰纹样开始被应用到建筑装饰中，如莲花纹、八卦纹等。贵族住宅往往使用庑殿式屋顶，屋脊上多饰以鸱尾，房屋的墙壁上多设有直棂窗。

唐代（618—907）是中国建

● 唐代佛教建筑：陕西西安荐福寺小雁塔
Buddhist Architecture of the Tang Dynasty
(618-907): Little Wild Goose Pagoda of Jianfu
Temple in Xi'an, Shaanxi Province

tail-shaped ornament and walls often equipped with mullioned windows.

The Tang Dynasty (618-907) witnessed the mature period of the development of Chinese wooden buildings. Architectural structure is perfectly integrated with art: the extra large brackets enabled the roof to look very far-reaching; pillars were thick at the bottom and thin at the top, which was in line with the aesthetic standards of the Tang Dynasty. In the Song Dynasty (960-1279), bricks began to be widely used during construction. Between the pillars of a residence emerged brick and wood structures and more attention was paid to the decoration than in the Tang Dynasty. The Northern Song Dynasty (960-1127) once had a provision for architectural decoration, saying that the average person may not use brackets or caissons and shall not decorate girders with colorful paint except palaces, official residences, temples and Taoist

- 宋代建筑墨戏堂
Ink and Opera Hall of the Song Dynasty (960-1279)

筑木结构发展的成熟时期，建筑结构与艺术达到了完美统一：斗拱十分硕大，使得屋檐显得十分深远；柱子下粗上细，符合唐代人以丰腴为美的审美标准。宋代（960—1279），建筑中开始大量使用砖，住宅的柱间开始以砖木为结构，而且比唐代更加注重建筑的装饰。对于建筑装饰，北宋（960—1127）时曾有规定，除宫殿、官员住宅和寺庙道观外，一般人不得使用斗拱、藻井，不得用彩绘装饰梁枋。不

temples. However, quite a few people did not comply with the provision.

Architecture during the Liao Dynasty (907-1125) and the Jin Dynasty (1115-1234) inherited the architectural style of the Tang Dynasty and retained some characteristics of Tang architecture. At the same time, influenced by the Song architecture, great attention was paid to detail decoration between columns. Architectural decoration had little development during the Yuan Dynasty (1279-1368) and most of the styles were

中国建筑装饰
Chinese Architectural Decoration

过，有不少人并不遵守这一规定。

辽（907—1125）金（1115—1234）时期的建筑承袭了唐代的建筑风格，保留了不少唐代建筑的特点，同时又受宋朝建筑的影响，柱间重视细节的装饰。元代（1279—1368）的建筑装饰没有太大发展，大部分建筑相当粗糙。

明(1368—1644）清（1644—1911）时期，一般住宅门内设影壁，在大门、屋脊等处多有雕饰及彩绘。地面铺方砖，室内用罩、隔扇等分隔空间。而紫禁城则是这一时期宫殿建筑达到顶峰的代表性作品，传统建筑的装饰也被发挥到了极致。

quite primitive.

During the Ming Dynasty (1368-1644) and the Qing Dynasty (1644-1911), there was usually a screen wall inside a residential door and carved ornamentation and color paintings on the door and the roof ridge. Square bricks were used to pave the ground and covers and partition boards were used to divide up interior space. The Forbidden City is a masterpiece exemplifying the climax of the development of palatial architecture during the period and the traditional architectural decoration was also brought into full play.

紫禁城

紫禁城是中国明清两个朝代皇帝的皇宫。明朝第三位皇帝朱棣在夺取帝位后，决定迁都北京，即开始营造紫禁城宫殿，至明永乐十八年（1420）落成。依照中国古代星象学说，紫微垣（即北极星）位于中天，乃是天帝所居之处，天人对应，因此皇帝的居所又称"紫禁城"。

紫禁城位于北京，现称故宫。紫禁城南北长961米，东西宽753米，占地面积达72万多平方米，有房屋9000多间。四面环有城墙和护城河，城墙四边各有一门，南为午门，北为神武门，东为东华门，西为西华门。紫禁城的南半部以太和殿、中和殿、保和殿三大殿为主，两侧为文华殿、武英殿，是皇帝举行朝会的地方，称为"前朝"。北半部则以乾清宫、交泰殿、坤宁宫三宫和御花园为中心，以及两旁的东西六宫，其外东侧有奉先、皇极等殿，西侧有养心殿、雨花阁、慈宁宫等，是皇帝和后妃们居住、举行祭祀和宗教活动以及处理日常政务的地方，称为"内廷"。

　　紫禁城宫殿都是木结构、黄琉璃瓦顶、青白石底座，饰以绚丽夺目的彩画，整体建筑风格雄伟、富丽堂皇。

● **皇宫紫禁城示意图**
Sketch Map of the Forbidden City

The Forbidden City

The Forbidden City was the Imperial Palace during the Ming Dynasty (1368-1644) and the Qing Dynasty (1644-1911). It was completed in the 18th year (1420) during the reign of the third Ming emperor Yongle who upon usurping the throne, had decided to move the capital northward to Beijing. According to ancient Chinese astrology, the Purple Forbidden Enclosure (i.e. the North Star) is located in the meridian passage where the Supreme God lives. Therefore, the mortal equivalent of the Supreme God, the emperor, should live in a residence called "Forbidden City".

The Forbidden City is located in China's capital Beijing, and was hence called the Imperial Palace. It is 961 meters long from north to south and 753 meters wide from east to west, covering an area of more than 720,000 square meters. It has more than 9000 houses. It is surrounded by a wide moat and a city wall with a gate on every side. At the southern end is the main Meridian Gate. To the north is the Gate of Divine Prowess. The east and west gates are called the East Prosperity Gate and West Prosperity Gate. The Hall of Supreme Harmony, the Hall of Central Harmony, and the Hall of Preserving Harmony are located on the central axis of the southern end of the Forbidden City. Lying on the two sides of the central axis are the Hall of Literary Brilliance and the Hall of Martial Valor. This is called the "Front Court" and used for ceremonial purposes. The northern end of the Forbidden City is called the "Inner Court" where the Palace of Heavenly Purity, the Hall of Union, the Palace of Earthly Tranquility and the imperial garden lie on its central axis. It also includes the Hall of Ancestral Worship and the Hall of Imperial Supremacy on the east and the Hall of Compassion and Tranquility, Yuhua Pavilion and Cining Palace on the west, making up altogether six palaces. The Inner Court is the residence of the Emperor, the Queen and the imperial concubines, and was used for holding ceremonies to worship heaven, conducting political activities and handling day-to-day government affairs.

The Forbidden City is of wood structure and features yellow glazed tile roofs, and a green whitehead base decorated with magnificent color paintings. The architectural style is majestic and splendid.

> 传统建筑装饰的特点

无论是官式建筑还是民间建筑，它们的风格特点在很大程度上是来源于装饰。装饰铸就了中国传统建筑富有特征的外观，让建筑更具有思想内涵和艺术性。从形态上划分，中国传统建筑可分为城池、皇家建筑、礼制坛庙、园林、民居、陵墓、寺庙、道观、塔、牌坊、桥梁等。这些建筑类别大多结构奇巧，装饰精美，形成了自己独特的形态和风格：以木材、砖瓦为主要建筑材料，平面布局具有一种简明的组织规律，建筑造型优美，装饰丰富多彩，同时特别重视与周围自然环境的协调。

色彩特点

中华民族是世界上最早懂得使

> Characteristics of Traditional Architectural Decoration

Whether it is the style of an official building or a civil construction, the characteristics are largely derived by decoration. Decoration gives birth to the characteristic appearance of traditional Chinese architectures and instills more ideological content and artistic nature into buildings. Judging from the forms, traditional Chinese architecture can be divided into city walls, royal buildings, ritual temples, gardens, civic houses, tombs, Buddhist temples, Taoist temples, towers, memorial arches, bridges, etc. Most of these architectural categories have exquisite structures and delicate decorations and have formed their own unique shapes and styles: wood and brick are used as the main construction materials, the plane layout is simply organized, the shape is elegant and

用色彩的民族之一，色彩文化是中国传统文化的重要组成部分。古人在很早就确立了色彩结构，以青、赤、黄、白、黑五种颜色为正色，并把它们与五行中的金、木、水、火、土相联系，把中国人关于自然宇宙、伦理、哲学的多种观念融入到色彩中。中国传统建筑以土木结构为主，建筑所使用的色彩极大丰富了建筑本身，并且具有深刻的文化内涵。金黄的琉璃瓦、朱红的门窗、白墙黛瓦以及五彩缤纷的彩画额枋，让中国传统建筑迸发了无限活力。

the decoration is colorful. At the same time, special attention was paid to the coordination of the buildings with their surrounding natural environment.

Characteristics of Colors

The Chinese nation is one of the first in the world to know how to use colors and color culture has become an important part of Chinese traditional culture. From time immemorial, ancient Chinese people established a color structure that treats blue, red, yellow, white and black as pure colors and correlates them with the five elements of metal, wood, water, fire

阴阳五行说

阴阳五行学说是中国古代朴素的唯物论和自发的辩证法思想。它认为世界是物质的，物质世界是在阴阳二气作用的推动下滋生、发展和变化，并认为木、火、土、金、水这五种最基本的物质，是构成世界不可缺少的元素。这五种物质相互滋生、相互制约，处于不断的运动变化之中。

The Theory of *Yin-Yang* and the Five Elements

The theory of *Yin-Yang* and the Five Elements is the naive materialism and the spontaneous dialectic ideas of ancient China. It holds that the world is material and the material world breeds, develops and changes under the influence of *Yin* and *Yang*, and that the five basic elements of wood, fire, earth, metal and water are indispensable in constituting the world. They reinforce and constrain each other and are in constant motion and change.

and earth. Various concepts of Chinese people about the natural universe, ethics and philosophy were integrated into colors. The main structure of traditional Chinese architecture is civil structure. The colors used on the architecture has greatly enriched the building itself and have profound cultural connotations. Golden glazed tiles, vermilion doors and windows, white walls, black tiles, and architraves with color paintings enable the traditional Chinese architectures to shine with vigor and vitality.

In ancient times, blue was commonly referred to as "cyan" which represents the position of the East. The blue color commonly used in architectural decoration is ultramarine, also called "*Yun Qing*" which is a brightly-colored blue. The dragon-head ornament and eaves tiles on the roof ridge were often painted in blue. Blue and pale purple were usually used together in the color paintings of buildings and have good decorative effect.

Red is almost the representative color of China. It symbolizes good luck, happiness, bravery and justice. The habit of loving red by ancient Chinese people can be seen everywhere in China, be it on a wedding night, after one's success

在古代，人们把较浅的蓝色称为"青色"，代表着东方方位。建筑装饰常用的蓝色是群青，也叫"云青"，这是一种色泽鲜艳的蓝色。屋顶上的吻兽、瓦当也常用蓝色着色，而且在建筑彩画中蓝色经常与青莲等色搭配使用，具有很好的装饰性。

红色几乎是中国的代表色，红色象征着吉祥、喜庆、勇敢、正义。古代的中国人，从洞房花烛到金榜题名，从衣着到住所，崇尚红色的习俗随处可见。皇宫建筑的宫墙、门窗、柱子、额枋以及民居的大门大都漆成红色，而斗拱、天花

Chinese Architectural Decoration

● 乾清门檐下漆成大红色，是皇家权威的象征
Eaves of the Gate of Celestial Purity is Painted Red, Symbolizing Royal Authority

等建筑构件的彩绘中红色的使用频率也很高。

在中国古代，黄色象征着权力、富贵、光明和智慧，黄色曾是皇族的专用色，黄色还代表着孕育万物的土地。北京天坛的祈年殿三重檐中的中檐便是象征着土地的黄色琉璃瓦。黄色本身还具有浓厚的宗教色彩，很多佛教建筑、寺院装饰都会用到黄色。

在传统建筑装饰当中，白色的使用频率不是很高，多用于墙壁，

in a government examination and from wearing clothes to decorating residences. Most of the walls, doors, windows, pillars and architraves of an imperial palace and the residential doors are painted red. In addition, red is frequently used in painting brackets, ceilings and other architectural elements.

In ancient China, yellow symbolizes power, wealth, light and wisdom. Yellow used to be exclusive to the royal family and represents the land that nurses all things. The Hall of Prayer for Good Harvests in the Temple of Heaven has

● 北京故宫奉先殿琉璃瓦覆顶
The Hall of Ancestry Worship in the Forbidden City Covered on Top by Glazed Tiles

● 上海玉佛寺黄色墙壁
Yellow Wall of the Temple of the Emerald Buddha in Shanghai

● 徽州古村落，纯净的白色
Ancient Village in Huizhou, Pure White

例如中国南方徽州民居的显著特征之一就是白色的墙壁。

在远古时期，中国人崇尚黑色，以黑为贵，在阴阳五行说中，黑色代表玄武，方位上象征着北方。民居、园林等建筑的屋顶常用黑色的瓦件即"黛瓦"（黛是一种青黑色的矿物颜料）进行装饰。在彩画当中，黑色的墨线则起到了很好的色彩过渡作用。

triple eaves, the middle of which is made of yellow glazed tiles, symbolizing the land. Yellow is also extremely religious and quite often used on Buddhist architecture and the decoration of temples.

White is not frequently used in traditional architectural decoration except for walls. For example, one of the salient features of residences in Huizhou, in southern Chinese, is white walls.

青绿色常被用于寺庙等建筑物的彩画当中，建筑装饰当中常见的还有竹青绿的琉璃瓦当、琉璃螭兽（中国古代神话传说当中一种没有角的龙）等。

• 绿色琉璃瓦当
Green Glazed Tiles

In ancient times, Chinese people advocated and valued black. In the theory of *Yin-Yang* and the Five Elements, black represents the God of the Northern Sky, black tortoise and is a symbol of the North. The roofs of houses and gardens usually use black tiles called "*Dai Wa*" (*Dai* is a bluish black mineral pigment) for decoration. In color paintings, the black ink line played an important role in realizing color transition.

Green is often used in color paintings in temples and other buildings. Bamboo green glazed tiles and a glazed *Chi* (a hornless dragon in ancient Chinese myths and legends) are also commonly seen in architectural decoration.

图案特点

传统建筑装饰中的吉祥图案凝结了中国传统文化的精髓，是中国几千年历史文化的缩影。从这些吉祥图案中，不仅能看到各个时代的建筑特色，还能看出宗教、民俗以及外来文化对中国古典建筑的影响。

建筑装饰用吉祥图案的历史，可以追溯到商周时期。那时的人们在瓦当上刻画各种吉祥图案，以求趋吉避凶。秦汉时期是中国传统建筑历史上的第一次高潮，帝王大兴土木，建筑装饰上使用的吉祥图案也逐渐增多。隋唐时，建筑装饰用的吉祥图案已形成了独特的风格，并影响到了周边其他国家。宋元时期的建筑更加注重吉祥图案的应用，呈现出活泼明丽的风格。明清两代吉祥图案题材丰富和使用范围广泛，花草树木、飞禽走兽甚至器物都被纳入吉祥图案。建筑装饰中的吉祥图案，既融中国绘画、书法、工艺美术于一身，表达了古人对美的认知和感悟，又具有极高的观赏价值，从而成为中国传统建筑装饰的显著特点。

Characteristics of Patterns

The auspicious patterns in traditional architectural decoration are a reflection of the essence of traditional Chinese culture and a miniature of thousands of years of Chinese history and culture. From these auspicious patterns, one can not only see the architectural feature of each era, but also the influence of religions, folk customs and foreign cultures on classical Chinese architectures.

It can be dated back to the Shang (1600 B.C.-1046 B.C.) and Zhou (1046 B.C.-256 B.C.) Dynasties when buildings were decorated with auspicious patterns. People then depicted various auspicious patterns on eaves tiles in order to protect the buildings from evil. The Qin (221 B.C.-206 B.C.) and Han (206 B.C.-220 A.D.) Dynasties witnessed the first climax in the history of traditional Chinese architecture. Emperors launched large-scale construction projects and architectural decoration gradually adopted more auspicious patterns. During the Sui (581-618) and Tang (618-907) Dynasties, auspicious patterns used for architectural decoration formed a unique style and influenced other neighboring countries.

按照题材的不同，建筑装饰图案可分为祥禽瑞兽、花木、器物、图文、人物等。"纹必有意，意必吉祥"，造就了各式各样内容丰富的传统纹饰。

祥禽瑞兽

在传统建筑装饰当中，祥禽瑞

The architecture of the Song (960-1279) and Yuan (1279-1368) Dynasties paid more attention to the application of auspicious patterns, demonstrating a bright and lively style. The subject matters of the auspicious patterns were enriched and used on a large scale during the Ming (1368-1644) and Qing (1644-1911) Dynasties. For example,

● 天安门前的华表

天安门前的华表既是装饰物，又是皇家建筑群的标志。柱上雕有一条龙，盘旋而上，身上龙鳞清晰可见，威武庄严。龙是中国神话传说中的一种神异动物，体长威猛，能腾云驾雾，会兴风降雨。龙被分为四种，即身上带鳞的蛟龙，有翅膀的应龙，头上无角的螭龙和头上有角的虬龙。中国传统建筑中常见的龙形图案包括团龙、蟠龙、坐龙、夔龙、双龙戏珠、鸱尾、云龙纹、草龙纹、拐子龙等。在中国古代，龙一般属于皇帝专用，象征着皇家权威、高贵，但是在民间龙是吉祥、喜庆的代表，常常用于寺庙、·祠堂等建筑上。

Cloud Pillar before Tian'anmen

The cloud pillar before the Tian'anmen is both an ornament and a symbol of a royal architectural complex. The column is carved with a dragon coiling its body up. The clear dragon scales make it mighty and solemn. The dragon is a miraculous animal in Chinese myth and legend. It is long and mighty and can mount the clouds, ride the mist, arouse the wind and cause the rainfall. The dragon can be classified into four categories, namely, scaled dragon (*Jiao* dragon), winged dragon (*Ying* dragon), hornless dragon (*Chi* dragon) and horned flying dragon (*Qiu* dragon). The commonly seen dragon-shaped patterns in traditional Chinese architecture includes the coiled dragon, the curled-up dragon, the sitting dragon, the *Kui* dragon, two dragons playing with a pearl, owl tail, cloud and dragon, the grass dragon and the *Guaizi* dragon. In ancient China, the dragon is usually used exclusively by emperors and is a symbol of royal authority and highness. However, the dragon is often used by folk to represent good luck and festive atmosphere in temples, ancestral halls and other buildings.

兽占据着重要地位，常用于石雕、木雕、陶塑等。祥禽瑞兽包括龙、凤、狮子、虎、麒麟、龟等，是人们祈盼平安幸福，禳除灾祸的象征，备受喜爱和推崇。

● 台湾敕建天后宫屋脊上的凤

凤凰乃百鸟之王，雄为凤，雌为凰，寓意着和平与美好。在皇家建筑中，尤其是清代多用于后妃居所。凤还有贤才逢盛世的意思，常见的凤凰题材主要有丹凤朝阳、凤戏牡丹、百鸟朝凤、龙凤呈祥、凤栖梧桐等。

Phoenix on the Roof of Taiwan Tianhou Palace Built at Imperial Command

The phoenix is the king of birds. The male phoenix is called *Feng* and the female phoenix is called *Huang*. The phoenix is a symbol of peace and beauty. In royal buildings, especially in the Qing Dynasty (1644-1911), phoenix patterns were used for the decoration of the residence of the Queen and the imperial concubines. The phoenix also has the connotation of talented people meeting the golden age. The commonly seen themes of the phoenix are "the scarlet phoenix flies towards the sun", "the phoenix plays with peony", "all birds paying homage to the phoenix", "the dragon and the phoenix bring prosperity" and "the phoenix dwells on Chinese parasol tree".

flowers, trees, animals and even utensils were included in auspicious patterns. The auspicious patterns in architectural decoration integrated Chinese paintings, calligraphy, arts and crafts to express the ancient people's understanding in beauty. These patterns boast very high ornamental value and have become a salient feature of architectural decoration.

Architectural decorative patterns can be classified into auspicious animals, flowers, trees, objects, graphics and characters according to different themes. The idea that "patterns must connote meanings of luck" has injected meanings into various traditional ornamentations.

Auspicious Animals

In traditional architectural decoration, auspicious animals hold an important position and are commonly used in stone carving, wood carving and ceramics, etc. Auspicious animals include the dragon, phoenix, lion, tiger, kylin and tortoise which symbolize people praying for peace and happiness and the elimination of disasters. They are much loved and respected.

浙江绍兴太师少师石雕

绍兴太师少师石雕，狮子表情生动，造型活泼，细节十分讲究。狮子，又称"瑞狮"，在宫殿、寺庙、宗祠、民居、园林中都比较常见，多成对摆放在大门前。在古人心中，狮子是权贵的象征，寓意神圣不可侵犯，同时又有镇宅驱邪、求得平安的寓意。常见的题材主要有狮子滚绣球、太师少师等。南北方石狮造型不同，北方狮子多威武，南方狮子多活泼。

Stone Carving Lions of Shaoxing, Zhejiang Province

The stone carving lions of Shaoxing in Zhejiang Province have expressive and animated faces and are delicately designed. The lion is also known as "auspicious lion" and is commonly seen in palaces, temples, ancestral halls, residential buildings and gardens and is usually placed in front of a gate in pairs. In the hearts of the ancient Chinese, the lion is a symbol of the rich and the powerful. It has a sacred and inviolable meaning and can also be used to keep away evil spirits and seek peace. The common themes are "lion frolicking with the festival ball", and "grand lion and little lion". Lion shapes from the south and the north are different from each other, the north being powerful and the south being active.

铜铸麒麟

麒麟，神话传说中的瑞兽，与龙、凤、龟并称为四灵兽。在宫殿、园林、民居等建筑中都使用广泛，在建筑贴面、砖墙、垂花门、天花、额枋等处也较为常见，寓意吉祥、太平、福禄。

Bronze Kylin

The kylin is an auspicious animal in Chinese myths and legends and is known as one of the "Four Sacred Beasts" together with dragon, phoenix and tortoise. It is widely used in palaces, gardens and residential buildings and commonly seen on building veneer, brick walls, festooned doors, ceilings and architraves. It means good luck, peace and longevity.

- 北海琼岛永安寺山门殿前的铜龟

人们把龟视为长寿的象征，与龙、凤、麒麟并列为四灵兽。龟可预测吉凶，《龟经》记载："龟一千二百岁，可卜天地终结。"龟背纹样还常出现在建筑的砖、石等构件上，起装饰作用。

Copper Turtle in Front of the Mountain Gate Hall of Temple of Eternal Peace on the Qiong Island in Beihai Park

The turtle is treated as a symbol of longevity and known as one of "four sacred beasts" together with the dragon, phoenix and kylin. The turtle can predict good or bad luck. According to *Turtle Classic*, a 1,200-year-old turtle can predict the end of the universe. Turtle patterns often appear on the bricks, stones and other components of the building for decorative purposes.

- 唐代石虎

虎是猛兽，古人认为虎是降伏妖魔鬼怪的神兽。早在战国时期，虎纹就被用来装饰瓦当。虎的石雕常被用于宫殿、园林、陵墓等建筑。其既能保佑家宅吉祥平安，又可消除灾病。民间又有"云从龙，风从虎"的说法，虎纹还寓意着风调雨顺、国泰民安。

Stone Tiger in the Tang Dynasty (618-907)

The tiger is a beast regarded by the ancient Chinese as a divine animal subduing demons and ghosts. As early as in the Warring States period (475 B.C.-221 B.C.), the tiger pattern is used to decorate eave tiles; tiger-shaped stone carving is often used in palaces, gardens, tombs and other buildings. Tigers can bless houses with good fortune and peace and eliminate the plague. In folk culture, it is said that "cloud is controlled by dragon and wind is controlled by tiger". Therefore, the tiger pattern also symbolizes good weather, peace and prosperity.

- 连年有余木雕

鱼，与"余"、"玉"谐音，象征着富余、财源滚滚，常见的题材主要有金玉满堂、连年有余、吉祥如意、鲤鱼跳龙门等。

Year-on-year Surplus Wood Carving

"Fish", "surplus" and "jade" are homonymic in Chinese, symbolizing surplus and constant fortune. The common themes are "great wealth", "year-on-year surplus", "good luck" and "carps jumping over the dragon gate".

- 福寿双全图案

蝙蝠，蝠与"福"同音，寓意着幸福美满、吉祥如意。建筑装饰当中的蝙蝠形象多经过美化。

Pattern of Happiness and Longevity

"Bat" and "happiness" are homonymic in Chinese, symbolizing happiness and good luck. Most of the bat images in architectural decoration have been beautified.

• 北京北海琼岛永安寺山门殿前的铜鹤

鹤是长寿的鸟类，在古代神话传说中是仅次于凤的仙禽，被认为是超凡脱俗的禽类。又因鹤的体态高洁、优雅，故成为文人雅士志向高远、不与凡夫俗子同流合污的品格的象征。

Copper Crane in Front of the Mountain Gate Hall of Temple of Eternal Peace on the Qiong Island in Beihai Park

The crane is a long-lived bird and an immortal animal second only to the phoenix in ancient myths and legend. It is considered to be extraordinarily refined. Being noble and elegant, it has become a symbol of virtuous character for ambitious and undefiled literati.

花木

以花草树木为题材的吉祥图案在古典建筑中最为常见。例如，被称为"百花之王"、"富贵花"的牡丹，被誉为四君子的梅、兰、竹、菊等。或者借用花木本身的吉祥寓意，或者利用这些植物的特征，组成了吉祥图案，较为常见的包括福寿三多、连中三元、榴开百子等。

Flowers and Trees

Auspicious patterns themed on flowers and trees are commonly seen in classical architecture. For example, the peony which is called the "King of Flowers" and the "fortune flower", and plum blossom, orchid, bamboo and chrysanthemum which are known as the "four gentlemen". Borrowing auspicious meanings of flowers and trees or using the characteristics of these plants, the commonly seen ones of which include "good fortune and longevity", "get the three highest literary degress in succession", "pomegranate revealing 100 seeds", etc.

- 北京北海延楼外檐上的国色天香彩画

  牡丹，中国特有的名贵花卉，雍容华贵，被认为是富贵的象征，又称"富贵花"。

  Color Painting of National Beauty and Heavenly Fragrance on the Roof Ridge of the High Building in Beijing's Beihai Park

  The peony is a rare and elegant flower unique to China. It is considered a symbol of wealth, hence its another name of "fortune flower".

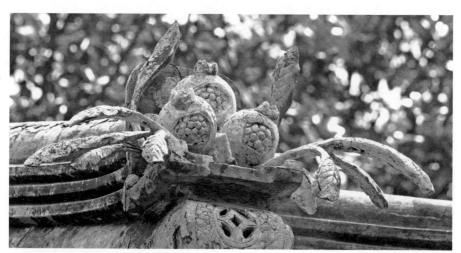

- 苏州拙政园建筑屋脊上的榴开百子

  石榴多子，古人视其为吉祥物，寓意多子多福、儿孙满堂。

  Pomegranate Revealing 100 Seeds on the Roof of Suzhou's Humble Administrator's Garden

  The pomegranate is a plant that produces numerous seeds and is seen as a mascot by ancient Chinese people, meaning "the more sons, the more blessings", "plenty of progeny".

梅兰竹菊木雕

梅，寒冬依旧盛开，能够忍受寒冷；兰，生于深林，不因为没人赏识而停止散发芬芳；竹，弯而不折，坚劲挺拔，四季常青；菊，秋季仍旧傲霜而立，品质高洁。梅兰竹菊并称为"四君子"，寓意着洁身自好、品行高洁、坚贞不屈、虚心正直。

The Wood Carving of Plum Blossom, Orchid, Bamboo and Chrysanthemum

The plum blossom is a plant still in full bloom in the cold winter and is able to endure it. The orchid originates in deep forests and emits a strong fragrance despite few appreciators. The bamboo can bend but not yield and remains green all year round. The chrysanthemum is a noble and virtuous plant that stands proudly against the chilly frost in autumn. Plum blossom, orchid, bamboo and chrysanthemum are collectively called the "four gentlemen", meaning that they are virtuous, unyielding, humble and upright.

器物

用寓意吉祥的器物组成吉祥图案，或借用谐音与其他物体组合成吉祥图案，是中国古典建筑中较为常见的吉祥图案形式。器物组合而成的吉祥图案，最常见的是博古图，它可以代表家族的文学修养或闲情逸致，常见于士大夫或达官贵人住宅的装饰。佛教和道教中一些

Objects

Forming auspicious patterns using auspicious objects, or combining auspicious objects with other objects with homophonic names are common forms of patterns in classical Chinese architecture. The most commonly seen auspicious pattern formed by objects is Diagram of Knowledge, which represents the literary accomplishment

寓意吉祥的法器也被纳入古典建筑吉祥图案中，如佛教中由法螺、法轮、宝伞、宝幢、莲花、宝瓶、金鱼、盘长等八种法器组成的八吉祥图案，道教中八仙手持的渔鼓、宝剑、花篮、荷花、葫芦、扇子、阴阳板、横笛等宝物组成的暗八仙纹等。除此之外，常见的吉祥图案还包括八宝图、聚宝盆、铜钱、琴、棋、书、画等，这些吉祥图案，代表着百姓们对美好生活的祝福。

- **苏州拙政园双钱纹铺地**

以铜钱纹装饰建筑很早就已经开始，铜钱也常与喜鹊、蝙蝠等组合成吉祥图案，最为常见的是铜钱纹花窗和铜钱纹铺地，寓意财源滚滚、衣食无忧。

Copper-coin-paved Floor in Suzhou's Humble Administrator's Garden

The copper coin pattern has long been used to decorate buildings. Sometimes copper coins will be used to form auspicious patterns together with magpies and bats. The most commonly seen are copper coin pattern windows and floors. They mean constant fortune and comfortable living.

and the leisurely and carefree mood of the family. It is commonly seen in the residential decoration of scholar-officials or dignitaries. Some auspicious objects used in Buddhism and Taoism are also included in the auspicious patterns of classical architecture. For example, the "eight auspicious patterns" include the charonia, Dharma Chakra, treasure umbrella, Buddhist stone inscription, lotus, Aquarius, goldfish and lucky knot. The dark pattern of Eight Immortals is formed by the bamboo percussion instrument, sword, flower basket, lotus, gourd, fan, *Yin* and *Yang* plates, flute and other treasures held by the Eight Immortals. In addition, the usually seen auspicious patterns also include the Figure of Eight Treasures, the Pot of Gold, coins, Zither, chess, calligraphy and painting, etc. They symbolize people's wishes for a better life.

● 山西乔家大院主楼雀替上的木雕博古图

博古图案是指包括瓷器、玉器、奇石、铜器等各种古器具，以及各种花卉、草木的装饰图案，常用于建筑及家具的装饰。其寓意清新高雅、超凡脱俗。

The Wood Carving of Diagram of Knowledge on the Sparrow Brace of the Main Building of the Qiao Courtyard in Shanxi Province

The diagram of knowledge pattern refers to the decorative patterns of various ancient objects including porcelain, jade articles, strange stones and bronze utensils, and a variety of flowers and trees. They are commonly used for the decoration of architecture and furniture. The Diagram of Knowledge pattern has a connotation of elegance and refinement.

文字

以文字为主的吉祥图案，其表现形式更加直接。如寓意福运当头的"福"字，寓意健康长寿的"寿"字，寓意喜事连连的"喜"字，以及回字纹等。还有，随着佛

Characters

The character-themed auspicious patterns have a more direct form of expression. For example, the word "*Fu*" which represents happiness and good fortune, "*Shou*" symbolizes health and longevity, "*Xi*" means the reoccurring of happy

教影响的扩大，佛教中的吉祥符号，比如卍字纹、盘长纹等也被融入到传统建筑图案中。

events and the pattern resembling the Chinese character "*Hui*"（回）means good luck. In addition, as the influence of Buddhism expanded, auspicious symbols of Buddhism, such as the swastika 卍 and the lucky knot were also integrated into traditional architectural patterns.

• **山西平遥古建筑门前影壁上的福字**

福字在中国传统建筑中甚为常见，无论是民间建筑还是宫廷建筑，常出现在门上或者墙壁上，寓意福运当头、福气临门，祈祷幸福、美满、吉祥。

"Fu" Character on the Screen Wall in Front of the Gate of Pingyao Ancient Buildings in Shanxi Province

The *"Fu"* character is most common in traditional Chinese architecture. Be it a civil or an imperial building, the *"Fu"* character often appears on doors or walls, meaning the coming of blessings and good fortune and expresses people's prayers for happiness and good luck.

人物

传统建筑装饰还常常以神话传说和历史记载的人物为题材，例如嫦娥奔月、牛郎织女、八仙过海、水漫金山、钟馗捉鬼、二十四孝等，寄托着人们对幸福生活的向往，以及教育子孙要孝敬父母、尊敬长辈等。

Figures

Traditional architectural decoration is also often themed on the characters of myths, legends and historical records, such as Chang E Flies to the Moon, The Cowherd and the Weaving Maid, The Eight Immortals Crossing the Sea, Flooding the Golden Mountain Temple, Zhong Kui the Ghost Catcher and the 24 Filial Exemplars. It carries people's expectations of leading a happy life, educating children, supporting parents and respecting elders.

● 苏州木渎古镇秀野竹堂上的八仙

八仙分别指铁拐李、汉钟离、吕洞宾、张果老、曹国舅、韩湘子、蓝采和、何仙姑，他们是指民间传说中的八位道教神仙。此题材寓意着神仙降临，长生不老的美好祝福。

The Eight Immortals in the Xiuye (Beautiful Field) Room of Mudu Town in Suzhou

The Eight Immortals refer to Iron-Crutch Li (Tieguai Li), Han Zhongli (Zhongli Quan), Lü Dongbin, Elder Zhang Guo (Zhang Guo Lao), Royal Uncle Cao (Cao Guojiu), Philosopher Han Xiang (Han Xiang Zi), Lan Caihe and Immortal Woman He (He Xiangu). They are eight Taoist immortals in folklore. The theme has a meaning of immortals visiting the mortal world and reflects people's wishes for longevity.

材料特点

由于中国传统建筑是以木结构为主，辅以砖、瓦、石等材料，所以根据建筑材料的不同，传统建筑装饰也运用不同的材料和方法，如石雕、砖雕、木雕、彩绘、灰塑、陶塑等。

石雕

石雕是建筑装饰中使用最广泛的品种。随着佛教传入中国，佛教建筑开始盛行。石窟、佛像、佛塔等都出现了很多石雕装饰。除了石

Characteristics of Materials

Traditional Chinese architecture mainly consists of wooden structures supplemented by various materials such as bricks, tiles and stones, etc. As a result, traditional architectural decoration adopted different materials and methods such as stone carving, brick carving, wood carving, color painting, plaster sculpture and ceramics according to the building materials.

Stone Carving

Stone carving is the most widely used kind of architectural decoration. With the introduction of Buddhism into China, Buddhist architecture began to flourish. Stone carving decoration began to appear on grottoes, Buddhist statues and pagodas. In addition to perrons, platforms, Buddhist seats, stone balustrades and decorated archways, ornamental columns, stone lions, stone tablets and stone buildings all featured

• 山西王家大院门墩——圆雕石狮
Door Mound of Shanxi Wang Family
Courtyard—Circular Carving Lion

中国建筑装饰
Chinese Architectural Decoration

台基、高台、须弥座、石栏杆、牌楼之外，还有华表、石狮、石碑、石幢等。后来，石雕被普遍用于建筑及其构件，石雕类别丰富多样，包括圆雕、浮雕、透雕等。

圆雕又称"立体雕刻"，即在各个角度都要进行雕刻。浮雕是在平面上雕刻出凹凸起伏的形象。透雕也称"镂雕"，即在浮雕的基础上，镂空其背景部分。

stone carving decoration. Later on, a large variety of stone carving was commonly applied to buildings and architectural components. These included circular carving, rilievo and openwork carving.

Circular carving is also known as "three-dimensional" carving, meaning that the engraving should be carried out at all angles. Rilievo refers to carving patterns of ups and downs on a flat surface. Openwork carving is also known as "through carving" which is to hollow out the background of a work piece on the basis of rilievo.

● 山西乔家大院建筑栏杆上的锦鸡牡丹浮雕
Golden Pheasant Rilievo on the Building Balustrade of Shanxi Province Qiao Family Courtyard

• 拙政园建筑屋脊上的丹凤朝阳石雕
Stone Carving of "the Scarlet Phoenix Flies toward the Sun" on the Roof Ridge of the Humble Administrator's Garden

砖雕

砖雕是模仿石雕而出现的一种雕饰类别，由于比石雕更加省工、经济，故在建筑中逐渐被采用。砖雕是由东周时期的瓦当、空心砖和汉代画像砖发展而来的，形成于北宋，被用做墓室壁的装饰品。明代，砖雕由墓室砖雕发展为建筑装饰砖雕，清代则是砖雕发展的巅峰时期。

Brick Carving

Brick carving is a type of ornamentation that imitates stone carving. It was gradually adopted over stone carving in buildings due to its labor-saving and economic features. It gradually developed from eave tiles and hollow bricks of the Eastern Zhou Period (770 B.C.-256 B.C.) and portrait bricks of the Han Dynasty (206 B.C.-220 A.D.). It took shape in the Northern Song Dynasty (960-1127) and was used as tomb wall decoration. In the Ming Dynasty (1368-1644), it developed from tomb brick carving to brick carving in wider architectural decoration. The Qing Dynasty (1644-1911) was the peak period for the development of brick carving.

画像砖

　　画像砖起源于战国时期，盛行于两汉，多用于墓室壁画，宫室建筑也有使用。画像砖主要用木模压印，然后经火烧制而成，也有的是在砖上刻出纹饰。画像砖画面的表现形式有浅浮雕、阴刻线条和凸刻线条。多数画像砖为一砖一个画面，也有一砖为上下两个画面的。题材内容多为播种、收割、舂米、酿造、盐井、宴乐、杂技、舞蹈，以及民间神话传说中的人物形象等。

Portrait Brick

Portrait brick originated from the Warring States Period (475 B.C.-221 B.C.) and prevailed in the Western Han (206 B.C.-25 A.D.) and Eastern Han (25-220) Dynasties. It was mostly used for tomb murals and sometimes for imperial buildings. Portrait brick is made by being fired after embossing with wood mold. Some are carved with patterns. The forms of expression of portrait brick are bas-relievo, intaglio engraving and raised engraving. The majority of portrait bricks are engraved with only one image but some are engraved with two images. The themes are mostly about planting, harvesting, husking, brewing, salt making, feasting, acrobatics, dances, and characters in folk myths and legends.

● 东汉时期的舂米画像砖
Portrait Brick Showing Husking in the Eastern Han Dynasty (25-220)

砖雕有两种做法，一种为"硬花活"，是用雕刻工具在特制的水磨青砖上直接雕刻而成；另一种叫"软花活"，纹样是用纸浆灰堆塑而成，制作方法不是雕刻，而是塑。砖雕一般用于门楼、影壁、祠堂、戏台、山墙、寺庙、牌坊等建筑的装饰，雕刻精巧，题材丰富。

There are two ways of making portrait bricks. One is "hard decorations" that are carved directly on specially-made blue bath brick using carving tools. The other is "soft decorations" whose patterns are made through molding pulps instead of carving. Brick carving is usually used on gate towers, screen walls, ancestral shrines, stages, gables, temples and monumental archways. It is exquisitely carved and rich in themes.

● 安徽黄山西递的门楼砖雕
Brick Carving on the Gate Tower of Xidi in Huangshan Mountain, Anhui Province

• 北京北海琼岛善因殿的琉璃砖雕佛像
Glazed Buddhist Statue in the Shanyi Hall of the Qiong Island in Beijing's Beihai Park

• 山西王家大院檐下的砖雕
Brick Carving Under the Eaves of the Wang Family Courtyard in Shanxi Province

• 墙上砖雕的植物图案
Plant Patterns of Brick Carving on the Wall

木雕

建筑装饰中的木雕，主要应用于木结构的房顶、梁枋、护栏、室内家具等，利用不同的木材质感进行雕刻加工，丰富建筑形象。据考证，殷商时期，木雕在建筑中就已出现。现存的建筑装饰木雕主要集中在明清时期的宫殿、寺、民居、戏台、祠堂等。这一时期，木雕几乎遍及了建筑的藻井、梁枋、斗檐柱、门、窗等各个建筑构件，题材多样，工艺精湛。

浙江东阳木雕、浙江乐清黄杨木雕、广东潮州金漆木雕、福建龙眼木雕，被称为"中国四大木雕"。

Wood Carving

Wood carving in architectural decoration is mainly used on wooden roofs, girders, guard rails and interior furniture. Different types of woods are used in order to enrich the image of the architecture. According to research, during the Shang Period (1600 B.C.-1046 B.C.), wood carving has been applied in buildings. The currently preserved wood carvings are mainly on palaces, temples, residential buildings, stages and ancestral shrines of the Ming (1368-1644) and Qing (1644-1911) Dynasties. During the period, wood carving was prevalent on the caisson, girder, eaves column, doors, windows and other building components themed on various subject matters and exquisitely engraved.

Wood carving of Dongyang in Zhejiang Province, boxwood carving of Yueqing in Zhejiang Province, gold foil wood carving of Chaozhou in Guangdong Province and longan wood carving of Fujian Province are known as the "Top 4 Chinese Wood carvings".

• 龙凤呈祥木雕
Prosperity Brought by the Dragon and the Phoenix

四大木雕

　　浙江东阳木雕约始于唐而盛于明清，自宋代起已具有较高的工艺水平，主要制作宫殿、寺庙、园林、住宅等建筑的装饰。东阳木雕以平面浮雕为主，有薄浮雕、浅浮雕、深浮雕、高浮雕、多层叠雕、透空双面雕、锯空雕、满地雕、彩木镶嵌雕、圆木浮雕等类型。东阳木雕的艺术作品一般不加彩绘，而是保留原木天然纹理色泽，格调高雅，又称"白木雕"。题材内容多为历史故事和民间传说。

　　浙江乐清黄杨木雕以黄杨木为雕刻材料，创始于宋元，流行于明清。题材内容大多为圆雕的八仙、寿星、关公、弥勒佛、观音等民间神话传说中的人物。

　　潮州金漆木雕最初是中国古代的一种建筑装饰艺术，之后逐渐形成一种木雕流派。其多以樟木或杉木为雕刻材料，加以生漆和金箔。雕刻形式有浮雕、立体雕和通雕等。

　　福建龙眼木雕是因雕刻材料为龙眼木而得名。龙眼木雕以圆雕为主，也有浮雕、透雕。题材内容多为寿星、渔翁、弥勒、达摩、仙女等，也有草虫、花卉、果盘和牛、马、熊、狮、虎及金鱼、仙鹤等。

● 浙江东阳木雕
Wood Carving of Dongyang in Zhejiang Province

• 黄杨木雕刘海戏金蟾
Boxwood Carving Liu Hai and the Toad

Top 4 Chinese Wood Carvings

The wood carving of Dongyang in Zhejiang Province began in the Tang Dynasty (618-907) and prevailed in the Ming and Qing Dynasties (1368-1911). A high level of workmanship was achieved since the Song Dynasty (960-1279). It was mainly used for manufacturing architectural decoration in palaces, temples, gardens, residential houses and other buildings. Dongyang wood carving is mainly flat relievo. It includes thin relievo, low relievo, deep relievo, high relievo, multi-layered carving, hollow double-sided carving, pierced carving, all-over carving, color wood inlay carving and log relievo. Generally speaking, work pieces of Dongyang wood carving are not painted in order to retain the natural texture and color of the wood. It is elegant in style and is also known as "white wood carving". Its themes and contents are mainly historical stories and folklore.

The boxwood carving of Yueqing in Zhejiang Province dates back to the Song and Yuan (1279-1368) Dynasties and prevailed in the Ming and Qing Dynasties. Like circular carving, its themes and contents are mainly figures in folk myths and legends such as the Eight Immortals, the god of longevity, *Guan Gong* (a famous general in the Three Kingdoms Period (220-280) renowned for his bravery and code of brotherhood), Maitreya and Kwan-yin.

The gold foil wood carving of Chaozhou, Guangdong Province, was originally an architectural decoration of ancient China. Later on, it gradually developed into a school of wood carving. Its main carving materials are camphor wood and cedar. They were coated with Chinese lacquer and gold foil. Its forms were relief, three-dimensional carving and hollowed-out carving.

The longan wood carving of Fujian Province was named after the carving material "longan wood". Its main form is circular carving, but also has forms such as relievo and openwork carving. Its themes and contents are mostly the god of longevity, fishermen, Maitreya, Bodhidharma, fairies, or grass, insects, flowers, fruit, as well as cattle, horses, bears, lions, tigers, goldfish and cranes.

中国建筑装饰
Chinese Architectural Decoration

• 清末金漆木雕隔扇门
Gold Foil Wood Carving of Partition Gate in the Late Qing Dynasty

陶塑

中国许多地区都有用陶塑装饰屋脊的风俗。例如，云南昆明农村地区的民居，在居所正中上方房顶安置瓦猫，用来镇宅。

Pottery Sculpture

Many regions in China have the custom of decorating roof ridges with pottery sculptures. For example, in the rural areas of Kunming city in Yunnan Province, a tile cat is positioned on the roof of the upper middle area of a house to protect it.

- **造型夸张的瓦猫**

瓦猫为蹲坐式，与一块盖瓦塑在一起。瓦猫的形象并不统一，有的像虎，有的像麒麟，还有的是"带飞翼"的虎，并附带有八卦图、圆镜、太极图等吉祥物。

Exaggeratedly-designed Tile Cat

The tile cat is in a squatting posture and molded together with a cover tile. The tile cats don't have a uniform image. Some look like a tiger while some like a kylin. Others are tigers with flying wings and supplemented with mascots such as the Eight Diagrams, round mirror and the Diagram of the Universe.

● 屋顶陶塑装饰
Pottery Decoration on the Roof

灰塑

灰塑是在福建、广东地区广为流行的一种屋顶装饰艺术，也叫"灰批"，就是用白灰和蚝壳灰为原料制成灰膏，然后用捏塑的方法做出丰富多彩的雕塑。灰塑可以制成浮雕或圆雕作品。灰塑的题材十分丰富，包括历史人物、吉祥题材、戏文故事等内容。在灰塑上加上五彩的颜色，称之为"彩描"。彩描是一种画塑结合的方法，就是先用灰塑技法做出装饰纹样，然后再进行彩画，常用来装饰屋脊和山墙部分。

Limestone Sculpture

Limestone sculpture is a widely-popular art form of roof decoration in Fujian Province and Guangdong Province, also called "Hui Pi". Emplaster is made by mixing the raw materials of lime and oyster-shell lime mortar and then kneaded by hand to make various colorful sculptures. Limestone sculptures can be made into works of relievo or circular carving. It has a wide range of themes, including the representation of historical figures, auspicious themes, skits and stories. Limestone sculptures can include various colors and be turned into what

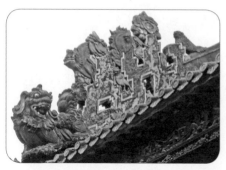

陈家祠堂屋顶彩描色彩鲜艳，雕刻精美，屋脊上的瑞兽栩栩如生。

colorful and exquisitely engraved color depiction on the roof and the lively auspicious animal on the roof ridge of the ancestral shrine of the chen family courtyard

is called "color depiction", which is a method of combining paintings with sculptures. First, decorative patterns are made adopting the technique of limestone sculpture and then they are painted with colors. Color depiction is usually used to decorate the roof and the gable wall.

● 广东省广州陈家祠堂屋顶彩描

Color Depiction on the Roof of the Ancestral Shrine of the Chen Family Courtyard in Guangzhou City, Guangdong Province

彩绘

　　传统建筑的彩绘在中国有悠久的历史，是传统建筑装饰中最突出的特点之一，其独特的风格、精湛的制作技术及富丽堂皇的装饰艺术效果闻名于世。"雕梁画栋"这一成语就是用来形容建筑物富丽堂皇的。

　　彩绘原本是为了防止木结构潮湿、腐坏、虫蛀，后来才开始突出其装饰性，宋代以后，彩绘已成为宫殿不可缺少的装饰艺术；清代，官式彩画则是中国传统建筑彩绘发展的全盛时期。彩绘有三大类：和玺彩画、旋子彩画和苏式彩画。

　　和玺彩画是清代宫廷建筑上最

Color Painting

Color painting on traditional architecture has a long history in China and is one of the most prominent features of traditional architectural decoration. Its unique style, superb manufacturing techniques and magnificent art effect is world-renowned. The idiom "carved beams and painted rafter" is used to describe a magnificent building whose beauty is attributable to color painting.

Color painting was originally adopted to prevent humidity, rot and bristletail, and used for decorative purposes later on. After the Song Dynasty (960-1279), color painting has become an indispensable decorative art for palaces. In the Qing Dynasty (1644-1911),

高等级的彩画，出现在明末清初之际。其特点是枋心用括线括起，枋心内画龙、凤等主纹。和玺彩画的主体框架线路一律采用沥粉贴金做法，不采用墨线；细部纹饰大部分也为沥粉贴金做法，故具有金碧辉煌的效果。因为宫廷建筑有严格的等级之分，所以和玺彩画也以纹样分为不同的使用等级。

枋心是檩枋中心，是梁枋彩画的中心部位。藻头，俗称"找

• 华丽的和玺彩画
Gorgeous Dragon Pattern

imperial color painting marked the prime time of the development of traditional Chinese architectural color painting. Color painting can be classified into three categories: dragon pattern, tangent circle pattern and Suzhou-style pattern.

Appearing in the late Ming (1368-1644) and early Qing (1644-1911) era, dragon pattern marks the highest level of color painting on the imperial buildings of the Qing Dynasty. Its feature is to attach vinculum to and draw patterns of dragon and phoenix on the central portion of the painted beam. The main frame of the dragon pattern adopts the method of gelled patterning and gilding instead of ink lines. Most of the detailed patterns adopt the same method, achieving a magnificent effect. Imperial buildings have a strict hierarchy, so dragon patterns are divided into different application levels.

The central portion of a painted beam is the center of girder color painting. The intermediate portion of painted beam refers to the part from the end to the center of the painted beam and is comprised of thong line, box, the intermediate portion and the end portion of the painted beam. The end portion of the painted beam is the color painting

头"，是指檩端至枋心的中间部位，由找头本身、皮条线、盒子、箍头等部分组成。箍头，是檩枋尽端处的彩绘线。盒子，是找头部分的一段小空间。皮条线，是五大线之一，亦是组成找头的一个部分。

line at the end of the purlin. The box is a small space of the intermediate portion of the painted beam. The thong line is one of the five lines and a component of the intermediate portion of the painted beam.

● 北京颐和园金龙和玺彩画

金龙和玺彩画是最高级别的彩画，只用于皇帝登基、理政的殿宇和重要的坛庙主殿。枋心以龙纹为主，以云气、火焰等为辅，枋心画二龙戏珠纹，藻头中青地画升龙，绿地画降龙，盒子中画坐龙纹，藻头较长时画双龙。

Golden Dragon Pattern of the Summer Palace in Beijing

The golden dragon pattern is the highest level of color painting exclusively used in palaces for emperors ascending the throne and administrating the country and in the main halls of important altars and temples. The central portion of the painted beam is mainly engraved with a dragon pattern supplemented by cloud, gas and flame. The central portion of the painted beam has the drawing of "two dragons play with a pearl" pattern; a flying dragon was drawn on the blue space of the intermediate portion of the painted beam and a descending dragon on its green space; the pattern of a squatting dragon was drawn in the box and twin dragons are painted when the intermediate portion of the painted beam is long.

箍头
the end portion of
painted beam

藻头
the intermediate portion
of painted beam

岔口线
the section line

皮条圭线
the thong line

藻头圭线
the section line

枋心
the central portion of
the painted beam

- 和玺彩画纹样的构成示意图
  Diagram of Dragon Pattern

- 北京天坛祈年殿龙凤和玺彩画

龙凤和玺彩画，级别稍低，主纹是龙、凤两种纹样，一般是青地画龙，绿地画凤。龙凤和玺中有龙凤呈祥、双凤昭富等纹饰。龙凤和玺彩画用于帝后寝宫和祭天的主殿，如天坛祈年殿。

Dragon and Phoenix Pattern in the Hall of Prayer for Good Harvests of the Temple of Heaven in Beijing

The dragon and phoenix pattern is of a low level with the dragon and phoenix being the main pattern. Usually, the dragon is painted on the blue space and the phoenix on the green space. There are characters of "prosperity brought by the dragon and the phoenix" and "two phoenixes bringing about wealth". The dragon and phoenix pattern is used in the sleeping palace of the emperor and the queen and the main hall for worshiping the heaven, such as the Hall of Prayer for Good Harvests in the Temple of Heaven.

● **体仁阁的龙草和玺彩画**

龙草和玺彩画，级别低于龙凤和玺，主纹是龙纹和大草纹，绿地画龙，红地画草。如大草纹中配法轮，又称法轮吉祥草，简称轱辘草。龙草和玺彩画用于皇宫的重要宫门和主轴线上建筑的配殿、配楼及重要寺庙的殿堂。

Dragon Grass Pattern in the Tiren Pavilion

The level of the dragon grass pattern is lower than the dragon pattern. Dragon and grass are the main patterns with the dragon pattern being drawn on the green space and the grass pattern on the red space. For example, the pattern that combines grass and Dharma Chakra can be called grass of auspicious wheel and wheel grass, for short. The dragon grass pattern is used on important imperial gates of the palace, the side halls and side buildings of architecture on the main axis and the halls of important temples.

其他用于宫廷佛堂建筑上的和玺彩画，主纹采用有宗教意义的梵文、宝塔河莲座等。

旋子彩画因藻头内画旋涡状的旋子图案而得名，其等级低于和玺彩画。在明代时，旋子彩画就已被使用，清代一般用于官署和寺庙的主殿、配殿以及牌楼等建筑。枋心部分和盒子部分可随着等级的高

Other dragon patterns used on the imperial Buddhist temples adopt Sanskrit and pagoda river rosette as the main pattern.

Named after the spiral roton pattern inside the intermediate portion of the painted beam, the tangent circle pattern has a lower rank compared with the dragon pattern. In the Ming Dynasty (1368-1644), the tangent circle pattern

低而变化，从高到低是龙纹、龙凤纹、凤纹、锦纹、夔龙纹、卷草纹和花卉纹等。

has been adopted. In the Qing Dynasty (1644-1911), it was usually seen on the main halls, side halls and decorated archways of government offices and temples. The central portion of the painted beam and the box can change as the grade levels differ. The levels from high to low are dragon pattern, dragon and phoenix pattern, phoenix pattern, mosaic pattern, *Kui* dragon pattern, curly grass pattern and flower pattern.

箍头
the end portion of the painted beam

盒子
box

箍头
the end portion of the painted beam

藻头
the intermediate portion of the painted beam

枋心
the central portion of the painted beam

• 旋子彩画纹样的结构示意图
Diagram of Structure of Tangent Circle Pattern

• 各式各样的旋子彩画藻头纹
Various Tangent Circle Patterns on the Intermediate Portion of the Painted Beam

- 旋子彩画，盒子纹

盒子是用于箍头之间的装饰纹样单元，因纹样的轮廓像一个盒子而得名。

Tangent Circle Pattern, Box Pattern

Box is a unit of decorative pattern between the end portions of painted beams. It is named due to its resemblance to a box.

- 旋子彩画，箍头

Tangent Circle Pattern, the End Portion of the Painted Beam

- 旋子彩画，旋花

  旋花是构成旋子彩绘的主要图案，在藻头内用旋涡状的几何图形构成一组圆形的花纹图案。因最外一层花瓣呈旋涡状，故名"旋花"。

  Tangent Circle Pattern, Spiral Flower

  The spiral flower is the main component of the tangent circle pattern. A series of round flower patterns is formed using spiral geometric figures inside the intermediate portion of the painted beam. The outer layer of the petal is spiral, therefore it is called "spiral flower".

旋子彩画也有等级之分，以用金量的多少作为分等级的依据。其中浑金旋子彩画在旋子彩画里等级是最高的，彩画部分全贴金箔，不做其他颜色。然后是金琢墨石碾玉旋子彩画。

The tangent circle pattern can also be graded according to different gold content. The tangent circle pattern of gold ranks the highest because its color painting is covered with gold foil instead of other colors. The tangent circle pattern of gelled patterning and gilding ranks the second.

• 北京故宫三大殿西庑房墨线大点金旋子彩画

Ink Line Gold Tangent Circle Pattern in the West Wing Room of the Three Grand Halls (The Hall of Supreme Harmony, the Hall of Central Harmony and the Hall of Preserving Harmony) of Beijing's Forbidden City

苏式彩画源于江南水乡苏州一带，明清时期传至北方并进入宫廷，成为官式彩画中的一个重要品种。苏式彩画主要用于园林中的小型建筑——亭、台、廊、榭等，以及四合院、垂花门的额枋上。南方气候潮湿，彩画通常只用于内檐，外檐则砖雕或木雕装饰，而北方则内外兼施。

The Suzhou-style color painting originates from the Suzhou area of the south of the lower reaches of the Yangtze River. During the Ming (1368-1644) and Qing (1644-1911) Dynasties, it was moved north to the palace and became an important type of palatial color painting. Suzhou-style color painting is mainly used for small architecture in gardens—pavilions, platforms, colonnades and pavilions on terraces etc., as well as the architrave of quadrangle dwellings and festooned doors. Since the climate in the south is humid, color painting is normally used on the inner brim. Decoration on the outer brim is brick carving or wood carving. However, color painting is adopted inside and outside the brim in the north.

• 北京颐和园建筑小额枋上的苏式彩画双燕图

宽大的荷叶上方，用红、白、绿色晕染出开得正艳的荷花，在荷的衬托下，双燕形象显得更加生动。

Suzhou-style Color Painting of Twin Swallows on the Architrave of the Summer Palace in Beijing

Above the large lotus leaf lies lotus flowers in full blossom painted in red, white and green. The lotus flowers set off the vivid image of twin swallows.

箍头
the end portion of the painted beam

箍头
the end portion of the painted beam

藻头
the intermediate portion of the painted beam

包袱
the semicircle pattern

藻头
the intermediate portion of the painted beam

• 苏式彩画纹样的结构示意图

Diagram of Suzhou-style Color Painting Structure

● 苏式包袱彩画

北方内檐苏画与和玺、旋子彩画相同，采用狭长枋心，外檐常将檩、垫、枋三部分枋心连成一体，做成一个大的半圆形"搭袱子"，俗称"包袱"。根据包袱内彩画题材的不同，可分为"花鸟包袱"、"人物包袱"、"线法套景包袱"等。

Suzhou-style Semicircle Color Painting

Like the dragon pattern and the tangent circle pattern, Suzhou-style color painting in the north adopted a narrow central portion of the painted beam on the inner brim and combines purlin, bolster and beam on the outer brim to form a large semicircle pattern. It can be classified into various types such as the flower and bird pattern, the figure pattern and the scenery pattern according to different painting themes.

● 北京故宫养心殿套景包袱苏式彩画

慈禧太后喜欢苏式彩画，内廷东西六宫、宁寿宫区的一些宫殿上均使用苏式彩画。

Suzhou-style Semicircular Scenery Pattern in the Hall of Mental Cultivation in Beijing's Forbidden City

Empress Dowager Cixi liked Suzhou-style color painting. Therefore, the entire six western and eastern palaces of the inner court and some imperial residences surrounding the Palace of Peace and Longevity adopt Suzhou-style color painting.

- 苏式彩画之套景包袱
  Semicircle Pattern of Scenery in Suzhou-style Color Painting

- 苏式彩画之人物套景包袱
  Semicircle Pattern of Figures and Scenery in Suzhou-style Color Painting

- 苏式彩画之花鸟包袱
Semicircle Pattern of Flowers and Birds in Suzhou-style Color Painting

- 苏式彩画之人物包袱
Semicircle Pattern of Figures in Suzhou-style Color Painting

- **北京恭王府花园苏式彩画**

  五福捧寿图为苏式彩画中最华贵的一种形式——金琢墨，工艺考究，用金多，画面精致。

  Suzhou-style Color Painting in the Garden of Prince Gong's Mansion in Beijing

  The diagram of "five happiness holding longevity" is the most luxurious form of Suzhou-style color painting. It uses a large amount of gold to produce a delicate image with sophisticated techniques.

- **海墁苏画**

  海墁苏画多用于次要部位，无枋心、包袱，梁枋的箍头或卡子之间画一些简单的花纹，是苏式彩画中的一般画法。

  Haiman Color Painting

  Haiman color painting is mainly used on less important parts such as the end portion of a painted beam without a central portion, a semicircle color painting or a girder and space between clamps. Usually, it is painted in simple patterns and is a general type of painting technique in Suzhou-style color painting.

● 金线苏画

金线苏画是最常见的苏式彩画，箍头线、包袱线等均沥粉贴金。

Golden Thread Suzhou-style Painting

The golden thread Suzhou-style painting is the most common Suzhou-style color painting. Gelled patterning and gilding are used on the lines for the end portion of the painted beam and for the semicircular pattern of the painting.

彩画不仅仅是一种文化艺术，更是一门需要极高技巧的工艺。建筑彩画装饰的基本步骤为基层处理、做地仗、刷油漆、作画四部分。不论是建筑中的桁、梁、枋、门板、隔扇、窗棂，还是精雕的斗拱、雀替，所使用彩绘，其技巧大致为以下四种：

沥粉、贴金：沥粉就是压挤粉浆，突出图案的线条。贴金就是把金箔用胶油贴在檐梁或木刻品上，有沥粉即有贴金，用金量越高，越

Color painting is not only a cultural art, but also a craftsmanship requiring high skills. The four basic steps of adopting color painting as architectural decoration are preparing the foundation, making the ground layer, painting and drawing. Be it a joist, girder, beam, door plank, partition board, window lattice or exquisitely-carved arch bracket and sparrow brace, the techniques of color painting used can be generally classified into the following four types:

Gelled patterning and gilding: gelled patterning refers to a technique of

能显示建筑的价值。

平涂法、色晕法：门板、隔扇等不画图案的部分，大都以大笔平涂的方式进行着色，色彩要求均匀。色晕是指色彩用深浅不同来表现，达到渐层的效果。

五彩遍装：依照不同图案的需要，使用胭脂、槐花、石青、石绿、朱砂等植物颜色，给建筑木构披上"华丽的外衣"。

水墨技法：在传统建筑的版墙上题字、作画。

squeezing slurry to highlight the lines of the image; gilding refers to the technique of sticking gold foil to beam or wood carving. Gelled patterning cannot exist without gilding. The gold content reflects the value of the architecture.

Techniques of flat painting and color-gradation: the technique of flat painting is normally used on spaces that do not need pictures, such as on a door and partition board. Color-gradation refers to the technique of expressing shades of colors to achieve an effect of gradational color stratification.

All-around color painting: based on the needs of different images, plant colors of rouge, pagodatree flower, azurite, malachite and cinnabar are used to cover the wooden architecture with a gorgeous coat.

Ink painting technique: refers to the technique of inscribing and drawing on the walls in traditional architecture.

传统建筑外部装饰
The Exterior Decoration of Traditional Architecture

　　中国人向来注重"天时、地利、人和"，崇尚自然，并与其和谐相处，中国传统建筑中直接与外部环境相关联的外部结构很好地体现了这一点。传统建筑的外部结构包括屋顶、墙、门窗、梁柱、台基、地面等部分，这些组成部分的装饰具有直观、鲜明的特征。

Chinese people always attach great importance to "favorable climatic, geographical and human conditions". They respect nature and live in harmony with it. As a direct link with the exterior environment, the exterior structure of traditional Chinese architecture greatly reflects the harmony between man and nature. The external structures of traditional Chinese architecture including roofs, walls, doors, windows, beams, pedestals and grounds have a direct and distinctive feature in terms of the decoration.

> 屋顶装饰

屋顶上的建筑装饰是传统建筑装饰中最重要的部分，具有很高的艺术价值。针对不同类型、不同等级的建筑，屋顶的装饰也有所不同。脊兽、瓦当、滴水、博风板、悬鱼、陶塑、灰塑、惹草等都是传统建筑屋顶的主要装饰构件。

脊兽

脊兽是中国传统建筑屋顶的屋脊上所安放的兽件，不同位置的脊兽有着不同的功能和寓意。传统建筑屋顶上安装的脊兽，其用途主要有三种：第一种是古人为求吉辟邪而设的吉祥物；第二种是对官式建筑而言，屋顶吻兽数量的多少，代表了殿宇等级的高低；第三种是防

> The Roof Decoration

The roof-top architectural decoration is the most important part and owns great artistic value. For different types and levels of buildings, the roof-top decoration is different. The ridge animal, eaves tile, drip channel, bargeboard, suspended fish, pottery decoration, plaster sculpture and triangle board are all major components of roof-top decoration in traditional architecture.

The Ridge Animal

The ridge animal is a decorative object placed on the ridge of traditional Chinese architecture. It has different functions and meanings when deployed in different places. Ridge animals on the roof of traditional Chinese architecture mainly have three functions: the first is to bring about good luck and keep away

水，脊兽本身就是专门设计制作的防水构件，如有的脊兽安放在正脊与四条垂脊的交会点上，而此处正是屋顶防水最不好处理的位置，脊兽起到了封固的作用，能够延长建筑物的寿命。

蹲兽，也称"走兽"、"仙人走兽"，是安放在宫殿建筑庑殿顶的垂脊上或歇山顶的戗脊前端的脊兽，分仙人和走兽两部分，其数量和宫殿的等级相关。每一个兽都有自己的名字和作用。还有一种走兽为跑龙，主要用在神庙正脊和亭子的垂脊上。

• 屋顶装饰
Roof Decoration

evil spirits; the second is to reflect the rank of official buildings judging from the number of zoomorphic ornaments on the roof; the third is to guard against water. The ridge animal itself is specially designed and manufactured to be water-proof. For example, some ridge animals are installed on the intersection of the main ridge and the four vertical ridges where it is the most difficult to resist water. The ridge animal serves the function of fixing and sealing, hence extending the service life of the building.

Squatting animals, also known as "running animals" and "immortal animals", are ridge animals placed in front of the vertical ridge of hipped roof palatial buildings and the angle ridge of gable roof palatial buildings. They can be classified into immortal beings and running animals and their number is related to the rank of a palace. Each animal has its name and function. There is also a running dragon which is mainly used on the main ridge of a temple and the vertical ridge of a pavilion.

● 河北承德须弥福寿寺殿顶铜跑龙

河北承德须弥福寿寺的铜质屋顶上有四条斜脊，共有八条铜铸跑龙。

Copper Running Dragons on the Roof of the Sumeru Longevity Temple in Chengde city, Hebei Province

There are four sloping ridges on the copper roof of the Sumeru Longevity Temple in Chengde city, Hebei province, and eight copper running dragons lying on it as decoration.

● 故宫太和殿

The Hall of Supreme Harmony in the Forbidden City in Beijing

• 故宫太和殿蹲脊兽

清代规定，骑凤仙人之后的蹲脊兽的数量为奇数，九为最高，如中和殿、保和殿、乾清宫，都是排列九个走兽。但为了凸显太和殿是故宫内最高等级的建筑，又增加了一个行什，这在中国宫殿建筑史上是独一无二的。

Squatting Ridge Animal of the Hall of Supreme Harmony of the Forbidden City in Beijing

The Qing Dynasty (1644-1911) issued an order that the number of squatting ridge animals behind the phoenix-riding immortal should be odd and nine at most. For example, the Hall of Central Harmony, the Hall of Preserving Harmony and the Palace of Heavenly Purity all installed nine running animals. However, in order to highlight that the Hall of Supreme Harmony is the highest ranking building in the Forbidden City, a decorative little animal called "*Hang Shi*" is added, something unprecedented in the history of Chinese palatial buildings.

⑨ 獬豸
Xie Zhi

④ 狮
lion

⑩ 斗牛
bull-headed
dragon

⑧ 押鱼
exotic fish

⑤ 天马
heavenly steed

③ 凤
phoenix

⑪ 行什
Hang Shi

⑦ 狻猊
Suan Ni

② 龙
dragon

⑥ 海马
sea horse

① 骑凤仙人
phoenix-riding
immortal

① 骑凤仙人，骑凤仙人被放于顶端，意为无路可走，只能骑凤飞行。

Phoenix-riding Immortal: placed on the top, meaning there is no alternative way other than flying a phoenix.

② 龙：传说中的神奇动物，能兴云作雨，是吉祥兽。

Dragon: a magical animal in Chinese legend that can cause clouds to gather and rain to fall. It is an auspicious animal.

③ 凤：即凤凰，传说中的鸟王，是吉瑞的象征。

Phoenix: king of birds in Chinese legend and a symbol of good luck.

④ 狮：传说中狮是兽中之王，是威武的象征。

Lion: king of animals in Chinese legend and a symbol of might.

⑤ 天马：神马，有翅膀可在天上飞行，用天马象征皇家的威德可通天庭。

Heavenly Steed: a divine horse that has wings and can fly. It symbolizes that the might and virtue of the royal family can reach Heaven.

⑥ 海马：名"落龙子"，造型近似天马，但无翅膀，而饰以火焰。海马象征着皇家威德可达海底。

Sea Horse: known as the "fallen dragon", is an animal resembling the heavenly steed. Instead of having wings, it has blaze as its decoration. It symbolizes that the might and virtue of the royal family can reach the sea bottom.

⑦ 狻猊：传说中能食虎豹的一种猛兽，形象类狮，有威武、百兽率从之意。

Suan Ni: a wild beast that can eat tigers and leopards in Chinese legend and resembles a lion. With its incredible might, it is the leader of all animals.

⑧ 押鱼：传说中的海中异兽，身披鱼鳞，有鱼尾，可兴云作雨、灭火防灾。

Exotic Fish: an exotic sea animal in Chinese legend with fish scales and a tail. It can cause clouds to gather and rain to fall. Its magic also includes fighting fire and preventing disasters.

⑨ 獬豸：传说中的独角猛兽，善辨是非曲直，古时以其作为皇帝"正大光明"、"清平公正"的象征。

Xie Zhi: a legendary kylin beast that is able to distinguish between right and wrong. In ancient times, it was a symbol of the fairness, honesty and justice of the emperor.

⑩ 斗牛：传说中的一种龙，造型是牛头兽态，身披龙鳞，遇阴雨作云雾，常蜿蜒道旁及金鳌玉栋坊之上，也是除祸灭灾的吉祥物。

Bull-headed Dragon: a legendary dragon with a bull head and dragon scales. It gathers clouds to generate rain and is usually found on the roadside or the Golden Turtle and Jade Rainbow Lane. It is also a mascot to prevent disasters.

⑪ 行什：传说中的一种带翅膀、猴面孔的神，挺胸凸肚，手执金刚杵，似在履行监押的任务。《清式营造则例》称其为"猴"。

Hang Shi: a legendary God with wings and a monkey face. It thrusts out its chest and holds a Vajra Pestle as if performing the duty of guarding the inmates. It is referred to as "monkey" in the *Building Standards of the Qing Dynasty*.

- 北京故宫雨花阁殿顶跑龙

中国古代重要的殿宇建筑物上还有跑龙装饰。故宫雨花阁的屋顶是铜顶，屋顶的4个转角上有4条跑龙。据清宫档案记载，4条跑龙共用铜720斤。民间礼制庙宇也有用跑龙为装饰的。例如，广东省五华县文庙的大成殿，殿顶正脊上有两条跑龙相对，曲身相斗，生动异常。

Running Dragon of the Tower of Raining Flowers in Beijing Forbidden City

There are running dragon decorations on important ancient Chinese palatial buildings. The Tower of Raining Flowers of the Forbidden City has a copper roof and four running dragons on the four corners of the roof. According to the archives of the Qing Dynasty, the four running dragons used a total of 720 *Jin* (360 kilograms) of copper. There are also private ritual temples using running dragons as decoration. For example, the Dacheng Hall of the Confucius temple in Wuhua County, Guangdong Province has two running dragons oppositely placed on the main ridge of its roof. It is so lively that it looks as if the two dragons are fighting each other.

垂兽，又称"角兽"，是垂脊上的兽件，为兽头形状，处在蹲兽的后面。垂兽多用琉璃瓦制成，长有双角，中间掏空用来钉入垂兽桩加以固定。其作用是防止垂脊上的瓦件下滑或被吹落，避免雨水渗漏，并加固与屋脊相交的部位。

Suspended beast, also known as "horned beast", is a decorative beast-head-shaped object on the vertical ridge sitting behind the squatting beast. Most suspended beasts are made of glazed tiles and have two horns. The middle of it is hollowed out for the fixing stake. The function of the suspended beast is to prevent tiles on the vertical ridge from falling, avoid rainwater leakage and consolidate the intersection of roof ridges.

Hip-mounted animal is an ornament on the hip ridge and used on gable and hip roof and double eave buildings. The shape of the hip-mounted animal is almost the same as that of the suspended animal which are all in a hornless dragon shape. However, the hip-mounted animal is generally known as the "beast head" and is slightly smaller than the suspended animal. The hip-mounted animal divides

戗兽是戗脊上的兽件，用于歇山顶和重檐建筑上。戗兽与垂兽的造型大体相同，都是螭龙之形，但是比后者略小一些，俗称"兽头"。戗兽将戗脊分为兽前和兽

长春宫屋顶上的垂兽和戗兽
Suspended Beast and Hip-mounted Beast on the Roof of the Palace of Eternal Spring

后。戗兽的数量设置有严格的等级制度，数量越多，级别越高，而且数目都是奇数。奇数表示"阳"，九为最大，故以九件戗兽等级最高。佛寺中大殿屋脊的戗兽数量一般为七或五。

the hip roof into the front roof and the back roof. The amount of hip-mounted animals is rigorously standardized. The more the amount, the higher the rank. All of the amounts are odd. Odd numbers symbolize "*Yang*", with nine being the largest. Therefore, a set of nine hip-mounted animals ranks the highest. The amount of hip-mounted animals on the roof ridge of temples is usually seven or five.

• **西夏时期无角琉璃套兽**

套兽是脊兽之一，安装于仔角梁的端头上，作用是防止屋檐角遭到雨水侵蚀。套兽一般由琉璃瓦制成，为狮子头或龙头形状。

Glazed Hornless Beast of the Western Xia Dynasty (1038-1227)

Glazed hornless beast is one ridge animal and is installed on the end of the son corner ridge. It function is to prevent the eaves corner from being eroded by rain. It is generally made of glazed tiles into lion-headed or dragon-headed shapes.

吻兽是房屋屋脊两端所装饰的瑞兽，在正脊两端的被称为"正吻"，又称"大吻"、"吞脊兽"等。根据形象的不同，正吻也有不同的称呼。唐至明清之前的建筑普遍采用鸱吻。鸱吻又称"螭吻"、"鸱尾"，为龙头鱼身，是龙生的九子之一，可喷水降雨，用来避免火灾。鸱吻除起装饰作用外，还可以严密封固两坡与瓦垄交会处，防止雨水渗漏。明清两代的正吻则通常用龙吻取代鸱吻，并且对吻兽的

Zoomorphic ornament is an auspicious beast used as decoration on the ends of the roof ridge. On the ends of the main ridge lies the "main ornament", also known as the "big ornament" or the "swallow ridge beast". The main ornament can be called different things according to different images. Architecture since the Tang (618-907) Dynasty and before the Ming (1368-1644) and Qing (1644-1911) Dynasties generally adopt an owl ornament decoration which is also called "hornless dragon ornament" or "owl tail-shaped ornament". It has a dragon head and fish body. It is one of the nine sons of dragon that can cause rain to fall in order to avoid fire. Besides serving as a decoration, the owl ornament can also fix and consolidate the intersection of two sloping tiles to guard against rainwater leakage. In the Ming and Qing Dynasties, an owl ornament is generally replaced by a dragon-head ornament and the usage of it is strictly regulated. Residential

● 龙头鱼身的鳌鱼装饰
Turtle Fish Ornament with a Dragon Head and Fish Body

使用有严格的规定。民居一般不允许使用大型龙吻，只有寺庙或官宅才允许使用，并以琉璃瓦质地为主。鳌鱼也是一种用于屋脊上的吻兽。鳌鱼，为龙头鱼身的形象，常放置于屋顶的脊梁两端，头在下，尾巴上扬。鳌鱼生于海里，有灭火之意，同时又寓意"独占鳌头"，即万事争第一。

buildings usually were not allowed to use large dragon-head ornaments except for temples and official residence where the ornament is made of glazed tiles. The turtle fish is also one of the zoomorphic ornaments used on roof ridges. The turtle fish has the appearance of a dragon head and a fish body. It is usually placed on the ends of the roof ridge with its tail curling upwards on the top. It is born in the ocean and is a symbol of firefighting. It also means championship, i.e. competing to be number one.

• 北京故宫太和殿龙吻
Dragon-head Ornament in the Hall of Supreme Harmony in the Forbidden City

• 苏州拙政园远香堂正脊上的鸱吻
Owl Ornament on the Main Ridge of the Drifting Fragrance Hall of Suzhou's Humble Administrator's Garden

龙生九子

龙，中国古代神话传说当中的神异动物，是原始社会时形成的一种图腾。龙生九子即龙生了九个儿子，龙承九子，子子不同（九是古代的极数）。

一种说法为：

老大囚牛，为龙头蛇身，平生爱好音乐；

老二睚眦，为豺首龙身，好斗喜杀，是龙子的战神；

老三嘲风，形似兽，平生喜欢冒险、张望；

老四蒲牢，形似盘曲的龙，平生喜好鸣叫、嘶吼；

老五狻猊，形似狮子，平生喜静不喜动，又喜欢烟火；

老六霸下，形似龟，平生好负重，力大无穷；

老七狴犴，形似虎，急公好义，仗义执言，能明辨是非，秉公而断；

老八负屃，身似龙，头似狮，平生好文，专爱书法；

老九鸱吻，龙首鱼身，口阔嗓粗，平生好吞，可灭火。

还有一说为：

老大赑屃，样子似龟，喜欢负重；

老二鸱吻，鱼形的龙，喜四处眺望，能够灭火；

老三狴犴，样子像虎，有威力，好狱讼；

老四蒲牢，形状像龙但比龙小，喜欢音乐和鸣叫；

老五饕餮，形狼，性贪吃，有首无身；

老六睚眦，形似龙有角的豺狼，嗜好杀戮，喜欢争斗；

老七狻猊，形状像狮，喜欢烟火，爱好静坐；

老八椒图，形似螺蚌，好闭口，性情温顺，反感别人进其巢穴；

老九貔貅，形似狮，有嘴无肛，喜欢钱财，只进不出。

Nine Sons of the Dragon

The dragon is a miraculous animal in ancient Chinese myths and legends. It is a totem created during the primitive society. The Nine Sons of the Dragon Legend refers to a story in which the dragon had nine sons, each of them different from the others (the number "nine" suggests a large number).

One saying is as follows:

The first son *Qiu Niu* has a dragon head and a snake body. It likes music.

The second son *Ya Zi* has a jackal head and dragon body. It is bad-tempered, fractious and inclined to fight. It is the god of war for the dragon sons.

The third son *Chao Feng* looks like a beast and loves to take risks.

The fourth son *Pu Lao* looks like a wriggling dragon. It likes to roar.

The fifth son *Suan Ni* looks like a lion. It likes tranquility, fire and smoke.

The sixth son *Ba Xia* resembles a turtle. It loves carrying things, hence is mighty and strong.

The seventh son *Bi An* is like a tiger. It stands for justice and can distinguish right and wrong and hear legal cases.

The eighth *son Fu* Xi looks like a dragon. Its head is like a lion's. It likes writing and calligraphy in particular.

The ninth *son Chi Wen* has a dragon head and a fish body. The bad-tempered beast likes swallowing things and can extinguish fires.

Another saying has it as follows:

The first son *Bi Xi* resembles a turtle. It loves carrying things.

The second son *Chi Wen* is a fish-like dragon. It likes to look out and can extinguish fires.

The third son *Bi An* is like a tiger. It is mighty and likes hearing legal cases.

The fourth son *Pu Lao* looks like a dragon but is smaller. It likes music and loves to roar.

The fifth son *Tao Tie* resembles a wolf. It is gluttonous. It has a head but no body.

The sixth son *Ya Zi* is a jackal with horns. It looks like a dragon and likes fighting and killing.

The seventh son *Suan Ni* is like a lion. It likes flames and sits quietly.

The eighth son *Jiao Tu* resembles spiral shells and mussels and tends to close its mouth. It is obedient and hates others intruding into its residence.

The ninth son *Pi Xiu* looks like a lion. It has a mouth but no anus. It likes money and prefers receiving to giving.

望兽，是一种屋脊兽件，位于房屋正脊的顶端。和吻兽朝内吞脊不同，望兽的兽头向外望去，故称"望兽"。望兽的等级不如吻兽高，常用于城墙上的城楼或商铺。

山花

歇山屋顶两端、博风板下的三角形部分即为山花。在明代以前多为透空，仅用悬鱼、惹草等加以装饰。明代的山花则多为砖和琉璃所制。明代以后多用砖、琉璃、木板等将山花的透空部分封闭起来，并在其上施以雕刻作为装饰，成为房屋装饰的重要部位。

The overlooking beast is a roof ridge decoration placed on the top end of the main ridge of the house. Unlike the zoomorphic ornament that swallows the ridge inwardly, the overlooking beast looks out, hence its name. The status of the overlooking beast is lower than the zoomorphic ornament. It is usually used on gate towers and shops.

The Pediment

The pediment refers to the triangular structure between the two ends of the gable roof and under the bargeboard. Before the Ming Dynasty (1368-1644), the pediment was usually hollowed out and decorated with suspended fish and grass. During the Ming Dynasty,

● 封闭式山花
Enclosed Pediment

宝顶

　　宝顶位于攒尖屋面的顶端，也称"绝脊"，多为金属或琉璃制造。其下部为砖砌线脚，上部为圆形中空的宝珠。形状有圆形、宝塔形和束腰圆形等。宝顶有防水和装饰作用，其形状、纹饰多种多样。南方园林的亭子攒尖顶端不放宝珠，而安置一些葫芦、宝瓶、仙鹤等砌筑雕饰构件，形式更为丰富多样。

most of the pediments were made of bricks and glazed tiles. After the Ming Dynasty, it was generally made of bricks, glazed tiles and boards. The originally hollowed out pediment was sealed and decorated with carvings to serve as an important component of architectural decoration.

The Precious Dome

The precious dome is located on the tip of the pyramidal roof and is also known as the "steep ridge". It is generally made

• 承德避暑山庄外八庙之小布达拉宫"万法归一"殿宝顶
"Little Potala Palace" of the Eight Temples outside the
Emperor Kangxi's Summer Mountain Resort in Chengde

of metal or glazed tiles. Its lower end is demolished brick and the upper end is hollowed round bead. It has circular, pagoda-style and girdle-style shapes. The precious dome can guard against water leakage and also serves a decorative purpose. It has a variety of shapes and patterns. Gardens in the south do not use a precious dome on the roof. Instead, carved ornaments such as gourds, bottles and red-crowned cranes are installed, showing more varieties.

悬鱼

悬鱼位于建筑屋顶两端的博风板下，垂于正脊，是一种建筑装饰构件，大多用木板雕刻而成。因为最初为鱼形，从山面顶端悬垂而下，所以称为"悬鱼"。悬鱼其实不限于鱼形，有各种各样的装饰形状，例如图像化的蝙蝠的形象，取"蝠"与福的谐音。由于悬鱼多出现在悬山顶、硬山顶的建筑中，而悬山

The Suspended Fish

The suspended fish is located under the bargeboard of the ends of the building's roof and is perpendicular to the main ridge. It is a decorative component which is mainly made of carved wood. Originally it was fish-shaped and suspended from the top of the mountain face, hence its name. In fact, it is not limited to fish shapes. It has a variety of decorative patterns such as images of bats, a

顶、硬山顶是中国民居的常用类型，所以其多应用在民用建筑中。

name homophonic with "happiness" in Chinese pronunciation. The suspended fish usually appears on commonly used types of civil buildings such as the flush gable roof and overhanging gable roof buildings. Therefore, it can be said that most suspended fish are used on civil buildings.

博风板

博风板又叫"博缝"，位于硬山式屋顶的山墙上部，为保护屋顶侧面的木结构而设。博风板多用木板，也有用方砖贴砌而成，有尖山式、圆山式、天圆地方式、铙钹式、琵琶式等。

• 山西平遥民居博风板
Bargeboard of Civil Buildings of Pingyao in North China's Shanxi Province

Bargeboard

Bargeboard is also called "*Bo Feng*" (seam). It is located on the upper part of the mountain wall of the flush gable roof building to protect the wooden structure on the side face of the roof. Bargeboard is mainly made of boards but sometimes built by laying square bricks. It can be classified into different styles such as peaked style, circular style, the "round heaven and square earth" style, cymbal style and lute style.

- 山西太原晋祠木悬鱼
  悬鱼寓意水，以避火灾。"鱼"又与"余"谐音，寓意生活富足。
  Wooden Suspended Fish of the Jin Memorial Hall of Taiyuan in Shanxi Province
  Suspended fish connotes water, hence it can be used to prevent fire disasters. "Fish" is homophonic with "surplus" in Chinese pronunciation, meaning an affluent life.

瓦当

瓦当，俗称"盖头瓦"、"瓦头"。中国古代建筑中的陶瓦是一块压一块，从屋脊一直排列到屋檐底端，处在众瓦之底的瓦就是瓦当，是屋顶的重要构件。瓦当的作用是保护飞檐避免受风吹、日晒、雨淋的损坏，延长飞檐的使用寿命。瓦当的种类很多，质地上分为灰陶瓦当、琉璃瓦当和金属瓦当；形制上有半圆形、圆形和大半圆形三种；纹饰上可分为图案纹瓦当、图像纹瓦当和文字瓦当三大类。

The Eaves Tile

The eaves tile is are also called "cover tile" or "dripping tile". In ancient Chinese buildings, ceramic tiles are laid one after another from the ridge to the lower end of the eave. At the bottom of the ceramic tiles lies the eaves tile, an important component on the roof. Its function is to protect the cornice from being damaged by wind, sun and rain to extend its life. Eaves tiles can be classified into many types. For example, in terms of the texture, they can be classified into ceramic tiles, glazed tiles and metal tiles; in terms of their shape, they can be classified into semicircular, circular and large semicircular; in terms of the pattern, they can be classified into tiles of patterns, tiles of images and tiles of characters.

• **夔龙纹半瓦当**

半瓦当是早期的瓦当形式，现存最早的半瓦当是西周遗存。瓦当上的夔龙造型简单，线条古朴，以直线构成夔龙纹的形象。

Semicircular Eaves Tile of *Kui* Dragon Pattern

Semicircular eaves tile is a form of early eaves tile. The earliest semicircular eaves tile in existence is from the Western Zhou Dynasty (1046 B.C.-771 B.C.). It has simple *Kui* dragon pattern and primitive lines. The *Kui* dragon pattern is drawn with straight lines.

- 黄琉璃龙纹瓦当

龙首居中，龙身随瓦当舒展，显得美观大方。

Yellow Glaze *Kui* Dragon Eaves Tile

The dragon head is located in the center. The body of the dragon stretches with the tile and looks beautiful and graceful.

- 汉代"长乐未央"文字瓦当

Tiles of Characters "长乐未央"
(endless joy) of the Han Dynasty
(206 B.C.- 220 A.D.)

- 青龙纹瓦当

Eaves Tile of Green Dragon Pattern

- 朱雀纹瓦当

Eaves Tile of Rosefinch Pattern

- 白虎纹瓦当

Eaves Tile of White Tiger Pattern

- 玄武瓦当

Eaves Tile of Black Tortoise Pattern

> 墙

　　在以木结构为主的古建筑中，墙体一般没有承重功能，只是起围合、保暖、避风雨的作用。墙的装饰方式主要包括墙体堆砌和砖雕。装饰性较强的墙主要有山墙、云墙、阶梯墙、虎皮石墙和粉墙等。

> **The Wall**

Among ancient buildings built primarily of wood, walls generally don't serve the purpose of bearing loads but provide enclosure, warmth and shelter from the wind and rain. The decoration of walls is mainly manifested in the piling of the wall body and brick carvings. Highly decorative walls include the mountain-shape gable, cloud wall, ladder wall, tiger-skin stone walls and whitewashed wall.

● 宫殿的铁红色粉墙
Iron Red Whitewashed Wall in the Palace

- 墙顶覆有小青瓦并有龙头装饰的云墙

云墙是园林中常用墙体形式之一，又名"波形墙"，即墙头做成起伏波浪形状，线条流畅轻快，富于韵律。墙面常抹白灰，墙头覆小青瓦。

Top of the Cloud Wall Covered with Small Green Tiles and Dragon Heads as Decorations

The cloud wall is commonly seen in gardens and also known as the "wavy wall" because its top is shaped like undulating waves in smooth and delightful lines with rich rhythms. The surface of the wall is often wiped with lime, while the top of the wall is covered with small green tiles.

- 虎皮石墙

虎皮石墙是中国传统建筑常用的一种墙体，以不规则的山石块砌墙，石块间以白灰膏勾缝，有凹缝、平缝、凸缝三种勾缝的方法，既形成自然的花纹，又显出石材的天然肌理效果，使墙体具有田园风格。

Tiger-skin Stone Walls

The tiger-skin stone wall is one of the most commonly used walls in traditional Chinese architecture. It is built of irregular mountain stones, with white plaster filling up the joints among the stones. The three styles of filling the joints in concave, flat and convex methods do not merely trace out natural patterns but also reveal the natural textural effects of the stone, giving the wall a pastoral touch.

• 墙头呈阶梯状错落的阶梯墙

阶梯墙，又名"马头墙"，常建于坡地，墙头呈阶梯状错落，做凸出线脚和小青瓦檐脊。其轮廓变化，高低相错，有很好的装饰性，可丰富园林风景的构图。

Ladder Wall with Ladder-like Patchwork on Top

The ladder wall, also known as the "horse-head wall", is often built on slopes. The top of the wall shows a patchwork-like ladder with embossed molding lines and eave ridges of small green tiles. Its varied outlines going up and down provide itself with good decorative effects, which enrich the scenic structure of the garden landscape.

• 南方园林的白墙

White Wall of a Southern Landscaped Garden

● 北方民居的青灰墙

粉墙，又叫"混水墙"，是进行抹灰、粉刷处理后的墙体。宫廷建筑的宫墙多为铁红色粉墙，南方民居多为白墙，北方民居多为青灰墙。

Greenish-gray Wall of Local Residence in North China

The whitewashed wall, also known as the "plastered brick wall", is a wall processed by plastering and whitewashing. Most of the whitewashed walls in palace buildings are iron red, while those in south China are white, and those in the north, greenish-gray.

花瓦顶是建筑院墙墙帽常采用的方式。墙帽的种类很多，用瓦砌成的常见的有蓑衣顶、眉子顶。有与屋顶相同的各式墙帽，还有花样很多的花瓦顶、花砖顶。其中花瓦顶就是在墙帽部分采用花瓦的做法，花瓦做法也用于园林的院墙、门楼、屋脊等处，有非常好的装饰作用。常见的花瓦图案有许多种，

The flower-tile top is a form of wall cap commonly adopted in constructing the courtyard walls. There are many types of wall caps. The wall caps made of tiles may be seen in walls with the straw raincoat top and the eyebrow-shape top, as well as the flower-tile top and the flower-brick top, which come in many various forms. The flower-tile top refers to the use of flowery tiles on the wall

如官式做法有沙锅套、十字花、锁链、竹节、长寿字、假叶子、银锭、料瓣花、辘轳钱等，这些基本做法还可以组合使用。

墀头是指硬山式建筑的山墙前后向外延伸，超出檐柱之外的部位。山墙是砌于房屋侧面的墙体，因硬山式建筑的山墙上部与屋顶相接处为"山"字形，因此得名。墀头在建筑里面比较显眼的位置，因此特别注重装饰。例如，北京四合院中的墀头装饰，题材内容非常丰富，大多为寓意吉祥的图案。

cap. It is also seen in garden walls, gate towers, house ridges etc. to achieve good decorative effects. There are many kinds of patterns for the flower tile, such as the official editions of the casserole cap, cruciate flower, chains, bamboo sections, longevity characters, fake leaves, silver ingot, *Liaoban* flowers and windlass coins. These basic patterns can also be used in combinations.

Chi Tou refers to the portion of the gable of the flush-gable construction that extends beyond the eaves columns in the front or in the back. The mountain-shaped gables are used as the side walls for a house. The mountain gable derives its name from the Chinese character for mountain because it connects with the flush-gable roof of the house and forms a shape similar to the Chinese character of mountain (山). Since the *Chi Tou* is located at a rather obvious position of a building, it is therefore particularly featured as decorative. For example, the *Chi Tou* decorations of the Beijing quadrangle dwelling feature plenty of themes and most of them are patterns with auspicious significance.

● 房屋山墙

Mountain-shaped Gable of a House

● 墀头

Chi Tou

影壁，在南方又叫"照壁"或"照墙"。其形态可以是一堵独立的墙体，也可以依附于其他墙体上。设置在大门之内，叫"内影壁"，设置在大门之外的，叫"外影壁"。

影壁由壁座、壁身、壁顶三部分组成，装饰重点在壁身部分，用色彩、泥塑、砖雕等进行装饰，内容有人物、花鸟、器物、文字等。而砖雕的部分主要为壁身中央位置，四角位置辅助装饰。

The screen wall or shadow wall, also known in the south as "lighting screen" or "lighting wall", is a type of wall that can either stand independently or be attached to other walls. When set within the main gate, it is called the "inner screen wall". When set outside the main gate, it is known as the "outer screen wall".

A screen wall is composed of three parts, namely the wall base, the wall body and the wall top. Decorations are focused on the wall body by means of coloring, clay sculpture and brick carving, with such contents as personages, flowers, birds, artifacts and Chinese characters, etc. Brick carving is primarily used on the central part of the wall body and also on the corners as auxiliary decorations.

• 上海玉佛寺影壁砖雕"万象更新"
The Brick Carving of "All Is Renewed in Freshness" on the Screen Wall in Shanghai's Temple of the Emerald Buddha

- 山西平遥砖影壁上的麒麟砖雕

The Brick Carving of Kylin Patterns on the Screen Wall of Pingyao in North China's Shanxi Province

- 砖影壁上大大的"福"字装饰

Large Chinese Character "福" (meaning luck) Used as a Decoration for the Screen Wall

- 北京颐和园文昌园影壁上的宝相花砖雕

The Brick Carving of Rosette Flowers on the Screen Wall of Wenchang Garden in Beijing's Summer Palace

- 北京颐和园仁寿门云龙纹砖雕

The Brick Carving of the Dragon and Cloud Pattern on the Renshou Gate of the Summer Palace in Beijing

琉璃影壁是宫殿、皇家园林、礼制坛庙所用，壁顶多采用庑殿式或歇山式，壁座采用须弥座式，壁身饰以龙纹。龙纹有一龙、三龙、五龙、七龙、九龙之分。中国现存有三座大型的琉璃影壁"九龙壁"，一座在山西大同明代代王府门前，建于明永乐年间，壁面阔近46米，是三座中最大的一座。另

The glaze screen wall is used in palaces, imperial gardens and altars and temples as specified in the ritual system. The wall top usually comes in the hipped-roof style or the gable and hip roof style and the wall base is the Buddhist sumeru seat, while the wall body is where the decorative dragon pattern rests. The dragon pattern may feature one, three, five, seven or nine dragons. There are

- ● 北京故宫皇极门九龙壁

皇极门是乾隆帝退位后的居所宁寿宫的第一道大门，地位非同一般。3500平方米的宫前广场南边，与皇极门相对的位置上，有一座面阔29.4米，高3.5米的五彩琉璃照壁，俗称"九龙壁"。壁下部为汉白玉石须弥座，上覆庑殿顶，壁面由270块彩塑琉璃砖组成。

Nine-dragon Wall at the Huangji Gate of the Forbidden City in Beijing

The Huangji Gate is the very first gate of Palace of Tranquil Longevity, where Emperor Qianlong resided after his abdication. It enjoys, therefore, a very unusual status. On the south side of the Palace's 3,500-square-meter front square, a multicolored glaze screen wall, commonly known as the "Nine-dragon Wall", is located just opposite to the Huangji Gate, measuring a surface width of 29.4 meters and a height of 3.5 meters. The lower part of the screen is the Buddhist Sumeru base made of white marble. With a hipped top, the screen's body surface was made of 270 colored sculptured glass bricks.

一座在北京故宫皇极门前，建于清代。北京北海公园北岸有一座琉璃九龙壁，是三座中唯一的双面壁，做工也最为精美。

currently three large-scale glaze nine-dragon screen walls in China. One is located in front of the Ming Palace in Datong, Shanxi Province, which was built during the Yongle Period (1403-1424) of the Ming Dynasty. It has a surface width of nearly 46 meters and is the largest among the three. The second one, built in the Qing Dynasty (1644-1911), is located in front of the Huangji Gate in the Forbidden City in Beijing. The third, located on the northern shore of Beihai Park in Beijing, is the only two-sided wall among the three. Its workmanship is also the most beautiful.

- ## 山西大同明代代王府九龙壁

明代古建筑。九条龙绚丽闪耀，昂首摆尾，盘绕弯曲，在海波上翻腾，犹如真龙再现，宛然如生。整个九龙壁面阔45.5米，高8米，厚2.2米。

Nine-dragon Wall of the Ming Palace in Datong, Shanxi

It is an ancient architecture from the Ming Dynasty (1368-1644). The nine dragons are represented in glorious splendor. With their heads held high, flicking tails and coiled bodies, they plough through the waves of the sea and look realistic. The entire wall of nine dragons has a surface of 45.5 meters in width, 8 meters in height, and 2.2 meters in thickness.

● 北京北海九龙壁

北京北海公园北岸有一座琉璃九龙壁，原本在一座庙宇——大圆镜智宝殿山门前，该庙被毁，现仅存九龙壁。此九龙壁建于清乾隆二十一年(1756)，壁高6.65米，厚1.42米，面阔25.86米，底座为青白玉石台基，上有绿琉璃须弥座。壁的双面各有用琉璃砖烧制的红、黄、蓝、白、青、绿、紫七色蟠龙9条，蟠龙戏珠于波涛云雾之中，形态各异，栩栩如生。九龙壁为庑殿顶，五条脊上共有龙32条，筒瓦、垄陲、斗拱下面的龙砖上都各有一条龙。如此算来，九龙壁上共有龙635条。整个影壁色彩绚丽，古朴大方，是清代琉璃建筑中的杰作。

Nine-dragon Wall in Beihai Park, Beijing

The Nine-dragon Wall in Beihai Park, Beijing was originally located in front of the main gate of the Temple of Grand Wisdom of Round Mirror before the temple was destroyed. The Nine Dragon Wall survived. Built in the 21st year (1756) during the reign of the Qianlong Emperor in the Qing Dynasty, this screen measures 6.65 meters in height, 1.42 meter in thickness and 25.86 meters in surface width. It is stationed on a greenish-white jade stylobate with a sumeru base made of green glaze. Both sides of the wall contain nine curled-up dragons in seven colors (red, yellow, blue, white, cyan, green and purple) made of fired glaze bricks. The lifelike dragons are depicted in different poses, playing with pearls in the clouds or in surf. The Nine-dragon Wall has a hipped top and a total of 32 dragons on its five ridges. Each brick under the round tiles, border ridges and brackets has a dragon on it. In other words, the wall has a total of 635 dragons. With gorgeous colors and primitive simplicity, this dragon wall is truly an architecture masterpiece of glaze work from the Qing Dynasty.

九龙壁

龙壁是一种传统建筑形式，九龙壁是最高等级。九龙壁是影壁的一种，通常建在帝后、王公居住或经常出入的宫殿、王府、寺院等建筑正门的对面。有砖雕、泥塑、彩绘、琉璃等多种形式。

Nine-dragon Wall

The dragon wall is a form of traditional architecture, and the Nine-dragon wall is the highest form of it. The Nine-dragon wall is a type of screen wall, usually built opposite to the front gate of the palace and estate where the emperor, empress, princes and dukes lived, or the temple and monastery that they frequently visited. It may be represented in many different forms such as brick carvings, clay sculptures, colored paintings, colored glaze and the alike.

● 清代黄木浮雕九龙壁
Nine-dragon Wall with the Relief on the Yellow Rafter Wood in the Qing Dynasty (1644-1911)

木影壁用木材制作，带顶子，立于宅院的二门之内，用两对夹杆石夹起的一面木制的板墙。木影壁的中部是艺术装饰的重点，有的采用木雕纹样，有的是采用吉祥文字。

The wooden screen wall is made of wood with the cap and standing between two gates in a courtyard. It is a board wall clamped by two pairs of clip stones. With a roof on top, the middle part of its facade is the focus of decorative art in the form of either wood carving patterns or auspicious Chinese characters.

中国建筑装饰
Chinese Architectural Decoration

• 太极殿五福捧寿纹木影壁
Wooden Screen Wall with the Traditional Five Bat Patterns and Longevous Pattern in Taiji Temple

• 老舍故居七彩木影壁
Seven-colored Wooden Screen Wall from Lao She's Former Residence

> 门

门的作用不仅仅在于出入，还有隔断内外环境空间的作用，同时也是居住者身份的象征。门又被称为"门面"、"门脸"，说明人们对门的重视。宫殿、宅院大门的建筑是门楼，一般也简称为门。门楼的造型、用料和做工代表了宫殿、

> The Door

The role of a door is not simply to provide entry and exit, but also to separate the space of the internal and external environments. It also serves as a symbol of status of the occupants. As the access portals, doors are also known as "door appearance" or "door face", which expresses the emphasis people

● **婺源江湾萧江宗祠正门门楼**

江西婺源江湾萧江宗祠为廊院式祠堂。有仪门、享堂、寝堂三进，正门门楼考究，门楼上装饰着精美的木雕图案。

Front Gate Tower of the Xiaojiang Ancestral Shrine in Jiangwan, Wuyuan

The Xiaojiang Ancestral Shrine in Jiangwan, Wuyuan is an ancestral shrine in the style of corridor yard. It contains three sections: the ceremonial gate, the offering hall, and the resting hall. The gate tower of the main entrance is exquisitely wrought with the door beautifully decorated with wood carving patterns.

宅院的社会等级。宫廷建筑、礼制坛庙、皇家陵墓的大门楼，往往是一组建筑群，并不是单一的门楼，民间的祠堂建筑也是如此。门楣、门板、屋顶等构件通常进行雕刻，运用圆雕、透雕等手法，雕刻出各种吉祥图案，以增加门楼的精巧与美观。门楼常用较为鲜艳的色彩进行重点装饰，门楼上的彩画都有不同的寓意，表达平安幸福、子孙满堂等美好心愿。

垂花门的檐檩下不置立柱，而改做倒挂的莲花垂柱，造型美观，民居、府邸、寺观、园林大都采

• 山西王家大院垂花门
Festooned Door of Wang's Courtyard in Shanxi Province

place on doors. The doorway structure of palaces and courtyards is known as gate towers, generally shortened as doors or gates. The shapes, materials and applied workmanship of a gate tower represent the social rank of the palace or courtyard. The large gate towers of palace buildings, ritual altars, temples and imperial mausoleums are often architectural groups instead of singular gate tower. This is also true with the architecture of ancestral shrines in civilian societies. The sense of sophistication and beauty of a gate tower will be increased by the sculpture work done in such parts as the lintels, door boards, roofs and other components of the gate tower. Through such techniques as circular carving and openwork carving, a variety of auspicious patterns are carved onto the gate towers. Gate towers are also highlighted by the decoration in bright colors. The colored paintings may carry various auspicious connotations, such as good wishes and prayers for peace, happiness, and productive household.

The festooned door is featured with the standing columns under the cross beam being replaced by two upside-down columns with lotus flower patterns hung in midair. Attractive in

用。古代所说的"大门不出，二门不迈"中的"二门"即垂花门。垂花门装饰性极强，各种装饰手段，如砖雕、木雕、石雕、油漆彩画均可使用，因此其在建筑、艺术方面的价值可谓极高。

垂花门外侧的梁头一般雕成云头形状，叫"麻叶梁头"，在麻叶梁头之下，有一对倒悬的短柱，柱头向下，头部雕饰出莲瓣、串珠、花萼云或石榴头等形状，酷似一对含苞待放的花蕾，这对短柱称为"垂花柱"，垂花门得名与这对垂柱有关。联结两垂柱的部件也有很美的雕饰。所有木构架上都有油漆彩画，以冷色为基调，间以五彩缤纷的小画面。

垂花门柱间安有雕刻精美的花枋，梁架上施以彩绘。门柱大体可分为中柱式和一殿一卷两种形式。中柱式即于面阔方向立柱，上安檐梁，以便承托上顶；一殿一卷式，则是在中柱式垂花门后接出一个卷棚顶，用立柱支撑，形成复合建筑。遂初堂前的垂花门为一殿一卷式。

洞门是指在墙体上开设的不

appearance, festooned doors are used in civilian residences, official mansions, temples, shrines and courtyards. The "second door" mentioned in the ancient saying of "Not exiting the main door, nor stepping out the second door" refers to the festooned door. Festooned doors are highly decorative. Almost all the decorative means, such as brick carvings, wood carving, stone carving and colored painting are utilized on festooned doors. Therefore, it has rather high value in architecture as well as in art.

The head of the outside beam of the festooned door is usually carved into the shape of a cloud, called the "Ma-leaves beam head" (*Ma Ye Liang Tou*). Underneath the Ma-leaves beam head are a pair of short upside-down columns with the heads of the columns facing downward and carved with various decorative shapes, such as lotus pedals, beads, calyx-like cloud and pomegranates looking like a pair of budding flowers. This pair of short columns is called the "hanging flower columns", which explains the name of the festooned door. The components connecting the two vertical columns are also beautifully carved. All of the wooden frames are painted with colored patterns based on cool colors

装门扇的门洞，可以砌成各种形状，如圆形、方形、瓶子形、葫芦形、海藻形、秋叶形、桃形等样式。洞门上端雕刻有海棠纹、回纹、云纹、角花等纹样。洞门多用于园林中的园墙之上，通过不同形状的洞门欣赏景物，可以获得不同的观景感受。

and sometimes supplemented with small fragments painted in riotous colors.

In between the doorposts of the festooned door are the square beams carved with flower patterns, with the beam frames color-painted. The columns can be generally arranged in the central-post style and the one-hall-one-roll forms. In the central-post style, the posts are set up in the direction of the *Miankuo*, with beams placed on them to support the top. The one-hall-one-roll form adds an additional round-ridge roof to the central-post styled festooned door, with the round-ridge roof supported by a standing post, thus forming a composite construction. The festooned door in front of Suichu Hall was completed with a one-hall- one- roll structure.

A caved door refers to an opening to a wall that does not have any door leaf installed. The opening can be in various shapes, such as a circle, square, gourd, seaweed, autumn leaf and peach. The top portion of the caved door is generally sculpted with patterns of begonia, fretwork, cloud, or angular flower. Caved doors are typically utilized for garden walls in courtyards. Looking through the variously-shaped caved door can allow viewers to experience different feelings from the landscape.

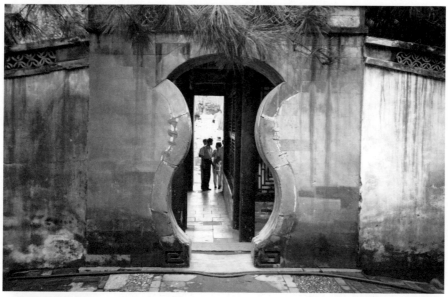

- 谐趣园瓶形洞门

Bottle-shaped Caved Door at the Garden of Harmonious Interests

- 海棠洞门

Begonia-shaped Caved Door

隔扇门也称"格扇门"，是安装在金柱或檐柱间的门，也是中国传统建筑最常用的门扇形式。隔扇门一般用于明间的装饰，整排使用，通常为四扇、六扇或八扇。格门的上部为隔心，由花样的棂格拼成，可透光。下部为裙板，不透光，可以有木刻装饰。还有的做成落地的长窗，即隔扇全用隔心而不用裙板。大片的空心窗格花纹产生极富变化的韵律感，裙板上丰富多彩的雕刻加强了房屋的装饰效果。

The partition door, also known as the "fan door", is a door installed between hypostyle columns or eave columns. It is the most commonly used door in traditional Chinese architecture. A partition door is generally used as decoration for the main room in the structural center of the house. It is typically used in a row of four, six or eight. The upper part of the door, called partition center, is made up of patterned window grids, which are pervious to light. The lower part, skirt board, impervious to light, can be decorated with wood carvings. In some cases, the whole piece is made pervious to light down to the ground like a long window, that is, the partition door is all partition centers with no skirt boards. A large piece of hollow patterned pane can produce a rich rhythm full of change and the variety of carvings on the skirt boards can enhance the decorative facade of the house.

● **安徽绩溪胡氏宗祠寝宫隔扇门**
胡氏宗祠寝宫与两庑的隔扇门形制相同，门上疏密有致的隔心，用于寝宫的采光。门的裙板上的图案为花瓶。隔扇门下是高高的门槛。

Partition Door at the Mausoleum of Hu's Ancestral Shrine in Jixi, Anhui Province

The partition door of the resting chamber in Hu's Ancestral Hall and those of its two side rooms are identical in form. The orderly arranged partition centers on the door provide the resting chamber with natural light. The skirt boards are decorated with vase patterns. A high threshold is used below the partition door.

门匾

门匾一般挂在门的上方、屋檐的下方，具有一定的装饰作用。古人用门匾表达经义、感情或表达建筑物名称和性质。横着的叫匾，竖着的叫额。匾额中有形如书卷之式的，称为"手卷形匾"，形式较优美，多用于园林小型建筑中，如亭榭、书斋等处的屋檐下或室内。匾额中有形如册页者，叫"册页形匾"，形式也很优美，多用于园林建筑。叶形匾是以一枚树叶之形为匾，是一种活泼的形制，多见于园林之中。荷叶匾即以卷荷叶之形为匾额，是一种少见的形制。虚白额即以透刻花纹为底的匾额，没有明显的底板，也叫"石光额"，大多用于园林中，是一种富有装饰性的匾额。

● **手卷形匾**
Scroll Plaque

The Door Plaque

A door plaque is generally hung above the door just under the roof. It has a certain decorative effect. Door plaques were used by ancient people to express comments, feelings, or the name and nature of their buildings. The horizontal door plaque is called "*Bian*", and the vertical one is called "*E*". Some of the door plaques come in the shape of scrolls with graceful forms, called the "scroll plaque", which are mostly placed under the eave or inside small garden structures, such as pavilions and studies. There are also some plaques in the shape of book pages called "page-shaped plaque" which are elegant in form and are often used in courtyard architectures. Leaf-shaped plaque is a vivacious design frequently seen in landscaped gardens. The lotus plaque is in the shape of a curled lotus leaf, which is a rare design. The white-blank plaque usually features hollowed-out patterns at its base with no apparent background plate, hence it also called "stone-light plaque". It is the kind of plaques rich in decorations, mostly used in landscaped gardens.

中国建筑装饰
Chinese Architectural Decoration

• 虚白形匾
White-blank Plaque

• 乾清宫"正大光明"匾
"Fair and Square" Plaque at the Palace of Heavenly Purity

• 北京故宫益寿斋蝙蝠如意匾
"Bats and *Ruyi*" Plaque of Yishou Study in the Forbidden City, Beijing

• 北京故宫怡性轩册页形匾
Page-shaped Plaque of Yixing Pavilion in the Forbidden City, Beijing

• 山西平遥乔家大院"会芳"荷叶形匾
匾额上有"会芳"二字，匾为绿色，字体贴金，十分典雅。

Lotus-shaped Plaque with the Chinese Characters of *"Hui Fang"* at Qiao's Family Courtyard in Pingyao, Shanxi Province

The plaque is green with gold-colored Chinese characters *"Hui Fang"* (Collection of aroma) in an elegant way.

门前装饰

在古代，不仅门本身的装饰极为重要，门前的装饰也很受重视，等级越高的建筑其门前装饰的等级也相应越高。门前的装饰主要门墩、滚墩石、拴马桩、上马石、石狮、铜铸饰品等。

门墩，又称"门鼓石"、"抱鼓石"、"门枕石"，常见于中国传统民居四合院的大门底部，起到支撑门框、门轴的作用。整体称门枕石，门外部分称为门墩。门墩上面一般都雕刻有精美的吉祥纹样。人们借助这些图案，表达了希望长寿、富贵、驱魔、夫妻美满、家族兴旺的美好心愿。

滚墩石常用于垂花门和影壁两侧，故又名"垂花门滚墩石"和"影壁滚墩石"。滚墩石的形状和门墩类似，不同之处在于滚墩石是对称的，从造型上看，滚墩石是一对门墩对接在一起。

古代民居门前的拴马桩埋立在大门前两侧墙根下，或者在院子里门旁并排伫立，柱头雕刻着狮子，又称"狮子柱"，也有雕成猴头、仙人、桃尖等形状的。拴马桩是北方独有的民间石刻艺术品。不仅可以用来拴马，还可以保护住宅墙面，不受碰撞。而且它和门前的石狮一样，既有装点建筑、炫耀富有的作用，同时还被赋予了避邪镇宅的意义。

上马石是便于古人上马的石台，用细青石或汉白玉石制成，有的上马石做成阶梯式，设置在大门前端，其上雕刻有各式各样的花纹、历史故事图等。旧时北方的

● **山西王家大院台阶边的抱鼓石**

抱鼓石上的《蟾宫折桂图》，是一个身穿状元服的人骑着马，身后有人举着华盖。

Drum-holding Stone by the Steps at Wang's Compound in Shanxi Province

The picture of *Plucking the Laurel Branch from Toad Palace* (a Chinese proverb implying success in the imperial examination) on the drum-holding stone shows an exam champion riding a horse, with people holding up a canopy behind him.

● 山西王家大院门前抱鼓石

雕刻的刘海戏金蟾，造型古朴大方。

Drum-holding Stone in Front of the
Wang's Compound in Shanxi Province

Carved with the motif of Liu Hai playing with
the golden toad, the stone is stylized with
primitive simplicity and open-mindedness.

● 山西太原晋祠门口的抱鼓石

Drum-holding Stone in Front of
Jin's Ancestral Shrine in Taiyuan,
Shanxi Province

府第和大四合院、大会馆的门前都放置上马石。住宅门前有没有上马石也是宅第等级一个划分标准。

石狮在宋代以前是帝王陵墓石雕，有辟邪和显示帝王尊严、权威的作用。元代以后，石狮使用范围扩大，宫殿、苑囿、官署等处均可使用，它成为门前建筑装饰的重要组成部分。石狮又是官阶等级的象征，古时规定：一品官员门前石狮头上的鬃毛卷为13个，称之为"十三太保"，二品官员门前石狮头上的鬃毛卷为12个，依次类推，七品官员门前的石狮头上的鬃毛卷为7个，但七品以下官员门前不准摆放石狮。

门钉最早用于板门之上，其主要作用是加固大门，后来逐渐演变成了装饰和等级的象征。明代时对门钉的数量无规定，一般是纵横三至五路，每路三至五

- 滚墩石
  Rolling Mound Stone

- 山西平遥建筑门前的拴马桩
  Horse Hitching Pole in Front of the Door of a Building in Pingyao,
  Shanxi Province

• 山西王家大院门前的上马石
Horse-Mounting Stone in Front of Wang's
Compound in Shanxi Province

枚。清代时，门钉的数量与建筑物等级有关，如皇宫大门纵横各九路，每扇门81颗门钉，象征帝王最高的地位。五品以下官府大门不准设门钉。

门簪安在街门的门楣之上，有两个或四个，形状有正方形、长方形、菱形、六角形、八角形等样式，正面用雕刻、描绘等手法饰以花纹、文字等图案。汉代就已经出现门簪，初时起到固定门扇的作用，后来其装饰性大于其实用性。门簪的图案以四季花卉较为常见，四枚分别雕以春兰、夏荷、秋菊、冬梅，图案间还常见"吉祥如意"、"福禄寿德"、"天下太平"等字样。两枚门簪时，则雕"吉祥"、"如意"等字样。

辅首又称"门辅"，是安装在大门上衔门环的一种底座，也是传统建筑大门上的一种装饰。在汉代，大门上就已经开始使用辅首，至今已逾2000年。民用的辅首一般安装在最主要的大门上，造型简单，多为圆形，铁制或铜制。帝王宫殿大门上的辅首等级较高，铜制鎏金，形象多为虎、螭、龟、蛇，寓意是星宿守门，能预知凶吉。也有用瞠目张口的狮头的，既有守门之意，又显示了皇家建筑的威严和庄重。

Decorations in Front of Doors

In ancient times, not only were the decorated doors extremely important, but the decorations in front of the door were also highly regarded. The higher grade the architecture, the higher the class of the decorations in front of the door. The decorations used in front of the door include the door mound rolling mound stone, horse hitching pole, horse-mounting stone, stone lions, cast bronze ornaments and so on.

The door mound, also known as "door drum stone", "drum-holding stone", and "door pillow stone", is commonly seen on the bottom of the main entrance to the traditional Chinese residential quadrangle dwelling. It is a stone component used to support the door frame and the

天安门前的石狮

北京天安门前的石狮，是北方石狮的代表，庄重威严，勇猛大气。

Stone Lions in Front of Tian'anmen

The stone lions in front of Tian'anmen are the typical northern stone lions with a solemn, dignified and majestic air.

午门的门钉

门钉一般用于实榻门（指由原木板拼接而成的实心大门，在大门中等级最高，体量最大）正面，起加固大门，防止门板松动的作用，更是一种皇家威仪的象征。

Door Nails on the Meridian Gate

Door nails are generally used on the front surface of *Shi Ta Men* (doors made of solid wood boards spliced up, which ranked the highest in class and the largest in body) to reinforce the door and prevent the loosening of the boards. Moreover, it was a symbol of imperial dignity.

door shaft. It is generally called the door pillow stone as a whole, while the portion outside of the door is called the door mound. The surface of the door mound is typically carved with delicate auspicious patterns. People make use of these patterns to express their hope for longevity, wealthy, exorcism, happy marriage, and family prosperity.

The rolling mound stone, commonly used on both sides of the festooned door or the screen wall, is also known as the "festooned-door rolling mound stone" or "screen-wall rolling mound stone". The shape of the rolling mound stone is similar to that of the door mound. The difference lies in the symmetry of the rolling mound stone. In terms of its design, a rolling mound stone looks like two drum stones put together.

The horse hitching pole in front of ancient people's houses were buried into the ground by both sides of the lower portion of the wall in front of the main entrance, or set up in a row by the side of the yard door. If the top of the horse hitching pole is carved with a lion, it is also called a "lion pole". It can also be carved with a monkey head, an immortal, or the tip of a peach. The horse hitching pole is a unique folk art of stone-carving in the north of China. Not only can it be used to tie horses, but also to protect the house wall from impact. Like the stone lions in front of doors, it decorates the architecture to show off the wealth of the residence and is also endowed with the significance of warding off evil influences and protecting the house.

The horse-mounting stone is a stepping stone used by ancient people to mount a horse with more ease. It is made of fine blue stone or white marble stone. Some are made into the shape of a ladder and placed in front of the door. A variety of patterns and pictures of historical stories are carved onto the horse hitching stone. The old northern mansions, large quadrangle dwellings and big meeting halls used to have

北京的四合院大门：门簪上有"吉祥"二字
Main Gate of the Quadrangle Dwelling in Beijing: the Door Cylinders Have the Words "Good Luck" on Them

- 北京恭王府花园怡神所垂花门的门簪
Door Cylinder on the Festooned Door of Prince Gong's Mansion in Beijing

horse hitching stones placed on both sides of the doors. The presence of a horse hitching stone also served as a grading criterion for the classification of the residence.

Prior to the Song Dynasty (960-1270), stone lions were used in the imperial mausoleums to ward off evil spirits and display the dignity and sovereignty of the emperor. After the Yuan Dynasty (1279-1368), the use of stone lions was extended to palaces, parks, gardens, and government offices. It became an important architectural decoration in front of the door. Stone lions were also a symbol of official ranks and grades. Ancient regulations required that the stone lions in front of the first-grade officials' residence should each have a total of 13 curled whiskers and were thus called the "thirteen heroic ones". The stone lions in front of the second-grade official's residence should each have a total of 12 curled whiskers. It goes on like this. The stone lions in front of the seventh-grade official's residence had a total of 7 curled whiskers, but officials lower than the seventh grade were not allowed to place stone lions in front of their residences.

Door nails were first used on large doors as reinforcement but they gradually became a decoration and a symbol of class. During the Ming Dynasty (1368-1644), there were no specific regulations on the number of door nails on a single door. Generally, it was generally three to five rows both horizontally and vertically, with three to five nails on each row. In the Qing Dynasty (1644-1911), the number of doornails was related to the class of the architecture. For example, the nine rows were set both vertically and horizontally in front of the Imperial Palace with 81 nails in all given to each door to represent the highest status of the emperor. However, officials below the fifth grade were not allowed to put nails into their doors.

The door cylinder is secured on the central threshold of street doors, used in twos or fours, and made in square, rectangular, diamond, hexagonal or octagonal shapes. Its front side is decorated with carvings, colored paintings or else in patterns of flowers, Chinese characters, etc. The door cylinder was already in existence in the Han Dynasty (206 B.C.-220 A.D.). It was initially used to fix the door leaf while, later on, its role as a decoration soon surpassed its practicality. Door cylinders are commonly patterned with seasonal flowers. When they come in fours, they may each feature orchid flowers for the spring, lotus flowers for the summer, chrysanthemums for the autumn and plum blossoms for the winter. Frequent patterns include phrases such as "good luck and happiness", "happiness, good fortune, longevity and virtue", "peace and harmony everywhere", and so on. In the case of pairs, words like "good luck", "*Ruyi*" (everything goes well), and others are often carved.

The door knocker ("head support" literally), also known as "door auxiliaries", is a base design installed onto the door to hold the knocking ring. It is also a type of door decoration used in traditional architecture. The door knocker has been used on doors for more than 2,000 years since as early as the Han Dynasty (206 B.C.-220 A.D.). Door knockers were used by civilians primarily on major doors. They were simple, mostly round in shape, and made of iron or copper. The door knockers used on the gate doors of the imperial palaces are of higher class. They are made of copper gilt with gold and generally shaped in the image of a tiger, hornless dragon, turtle, or snake to symbolize the zodiac guardians that can predict good luck and misfortune. There are also door knockers in the shape of a staring and open-mouthed lion to represent the gatekeeper and signify the majesty and solemnity of imperial buildings.

● 北京故宫景运门上的辅首

故宫大门的辅首为椒图形象，眼睛、鼻子以及眉毛上的装饰刻画细腻，图案使得辅首大气十足。

Door Knockers on the Door of Jingyun Gate in the Forbidden City, Beijing

The door knocker on the door of Jingyun Gate in the Forbidden City is delicately carved with the decorative image of *Jiao Tu* (one of the nine mythical sons of a dragon) with detailed and vivid depictions of the eyes, nose and eyebrows, giving it a majestic air.

门神

Door Gods

门神是道教和民间共同信仰的守卫门户的神灵。旧时人们都将其神像贴于门上，用以驱邪辟鬼，保卫家宅平安，祈求功名吉祥等，是民间最受人们欢迎的保护神之一。门神画是旧时农历新年贴于门上的一种画类，春节时可将宅院装点一新。

The door god denotes a belief in a divine door-guardian shared by Taoism and the general public. In ancient times, people would paste pictures of the door god on doors to ward off evil spirits, protect the safety of the house and pray for success, fame and good luck. It is one of the most popular gods in the world of the general public. Paintings of door gods were also posted on doors during the Lunar New Year Festival in ancient times as a kind of decoration in spring.

门神秦琼、尉迟恭

秦琼和尉迟恭都是唐代初期著名大将。相传唐太宗（599—649）在晚上睡觉时常常听到卧房外边鬼魅呼叫，抛砖掷瓦，故而夜不成眠。于是他便与众臣商议后，令秦琼与尉迟恭二人把守宫门，夜晚果然平安无事。后来唐太宗感念二人辛劳，于是将二人的画像贴在门上，照样管用。民间也开始流行贴二人画像在门上。

The Door Gods Qin Qiong and Yuchi Gong
Qin Qiong and Yuchi Gong were both well-known generals from the early Tang Dynasty (618-907). According to legend, Emperor Tang Taizong (599-649) often heard ghosts calling and throwing bricks and tiles outside his chamber while he was trying to sleep, which caused him could not sleep well. After consulting the officials in his court, he ordered Qin Qiong and Yuchi Gong to guard the gate to the imperial harem. Sure enough, the nights went by safe and sound disapperd ever after. Later, as a thankful repayment for the labor of the two generals, Emperor Tang Taizhong chose to paste the portraits of the two generals on the door and it was just as effective. Subsequently, pasting the portraits of the two generals also became popular among ordinary people.

门神神荼、郁垒

神荼、郁垒是传说中可以捉鬼的神。如果有恶鬼想要祸害人间，神荼、郁垒便会将其抓住喂老虎。古人在辞旧迎新之际，在桃木板上分别写"神荼"、"郁垒"二神的名字，或者用纸画上二神的图像，悬挂、嵌缀或者张贴于门首，意在祈福灭祸。

- 漳州年画《门神》（明代）

右为尉迟恭，左为秦琼。尉迟恭纯朴忠厚，勇武善战，一生戎马，屡立战功。秦琼勇猛彪悍，每战必先，常于千军万马之中取敌将首级。

Zhangzhou New Year Pictures Representing Door Gods (Ming Dynasty, 1368-1644)

The general on the right is Yuchi Gong, and the other on the left is Qin Qiong. A simple and honest man, Yuchi had proved his gallantry and superb fighting skills in numerous battles throughout his life and rendered illustrious military service. Qin, brave and fierce, led the charge in every battle and often dashed into the crowd of the enemy and chopped off their commander's head.

The Door Gods Shen Tu and Yu Lei

Legend has it that Shen Tu and Yu Lei were the gods who capture ghosts. If a malicious ghost tried to disturb the human world, Shen Tu and Yu Lei would capture it and feed it to a tiger. During the Chinese New Year when people were bidding farewell to the old time and welcoming the new year in ancient times, people would write the names of "Shen Tu" and "Yu Lei" on mahogany boards separately, or draw the images of the two gods on paper, and then either hang, embed, or post them on the door as a prayer to wish for a blessing and to fend off evil.

门神哼哈二将

哼哈二将为守护寺庙的两位神将，形象威武凶猛。一名神将叫郑伦，能鼻哼白气制敌；一名神将叫陈奇，能口哈黄气擒将。

The Door Gods General Heng and General Ha

General Heng and General Ha are the guardian gods of temples who had a mighty and ferocious appearance. General Heng's real name is Zheng Lun, who can release white gas through his nostril to subdue the enemy, and General Ha, real name being Chen Qi, can release yellow gas from his mouth to capture the enemy.

• 安徽绩溪龙川胡氏宗祠门上的神荼和郁垒

Images of Shen Tu and Yu Lei on Hu's Ancestral Shrine at Longchuan Village, Jixi County, Anhui Province

> 窗

窗是安装在建筑物上用来采光、换气的构件。传统建筑中的窗分两大类，一类是木棂格窗，在工艺上属于木作装饰；一类叫牖，是

• 灯笼框窗棂格
Grid Pattern Window of Lantern-frame Patterns

> The Window

The Window is installed in architecture to allow in lighting and ventilation. In traditional architecture, windows are divided into two categories. One is the wood grid-patterned window, which is considered decorative woodwork in industrial art. The other is *You* (windows between the room and the hall), an opening in the wall that is considered part of the masonry.

The wood grid-patterned window was the most extensively used window in ancient times. Since there was no glass in ancient China, the only way to solve the problem of indoor lighting and maintaining warmth was to glue paper onto windows. To ensure enough strength in window paper, the gridded-patterned window was utilized. Aside from being practical, grid-patterned windows also

在墙上开窗，在工艺上属于瓦作。

　　木棂格窗是古代广泛使用的窗户类型，中国古代没有玻璃，解决室内采光和保暖问题的唯一的办法是在窗上糊纸。为确保窗户纸具有一定强度，故普遍采用棂格窗。棂格窗除实用外，上面雕刻的不同样式的纹样，还可起到装饰作用。

　　镶嵌在隔扇、槛窗中的棂格子，用攒斗法拼成，式样很多，有龟背锦格、灯笼框格、冰裂纹格、

played a decorative role when engraved with various types of patterns.

The grid pattern set in the partition doors and the caged-in windows is built by using *Cuan* (a method of assembling small vertical and horizontal wood pieces into geometrical patterns through mortise and tenon joints) and *Dou* (a method of assembling small sculptured pieces into patterns) into various styles, such as brocade grids in turtle-shell shapes, lantern-frame grids, ice-

● 步步锦窗棂格
Window of *Bu Bu Jin* (Steps of Prospect) Rectangular Grids

● 古钱菱花棂格
Grids of Ancient Coin and Four-rhombus Patterns

- 支摘窗
  Removable Window

- 长春宫体元殿的支摘窗
  支摘窗上部可依天气变化用纱、纸糊饰，下部安装玻璃，以利室内采光。

  Removable Window of the Hall of All-encompassing Universe at the Palace of Eternal Spring

  The upper part of the removable window can either be pasted with gauze or paper according to the weather and the lower part is usually installed with glass to allow in light.

玻璃屉格、套方格、拐子锦格、盘长格、方眼格、豆腐块格、如意锦格、卧蚕锦格、四菱花格等。窗棂格花纹寓意美好，以象征的手法表现了人们对平安、幸福、欢乐、美满生活的向往，是中国门窗装饰构件中最精彩的部分。

crack grids, glass-tray grids, square-set grids, brocade grids in cane shapes, Buddhist lucky pattern grids, square-eye grids, tofu-block grids, brocade grids in *Ruyi* shapes, brocade grids of sleeping silkworm, four-rhombus grids, and so on. The grid pattern of windows bears beneficial implications in representing in a symbolic way people's longing for peace, happiness, joyfulness and a fulfilled life. It is the most exciting part of the Chinese outdoor decoration of doors and windows.

● 北京北海琼岛半月城智珠殿槛窗

槛窗安在槛墙之上、柱子之间，上下有转轴，便于开启和关闭。槛窗的设立有利于室内的透气、采光，增加建筑的通透性。槛窗的形式庄重，一般用于厅堂或园林等重要建筑中。

Caged-in Windows at Zhizhu Palace Located in Banyue City, Beihai Qiong Island, Beijing

The caged-in or framed window is installed above the caged-in wall and in between pillars. With shafts at the top and the bottom, it can be easily opened or closed. The caged-in window is designed to provide indoor lighting and ventilation and to increase the permeability of a building. The dignified style of the caged-in window is generally expressed in such important structures as halls and courtyards.

● 冰裂纹窗棂格
Grid Pattern Window of Ice-crack Patterns

● 四菱花棂格
Four-rhombus Pattern Grids

● 承启楼内直棂窗

直棂窗是一种古代常用的窗户类型，造型比较简单。圆形土楼的窗户一般都是直棂窗，这样的窗户通风性极好。其次，圆形土楼窗前一般是通道、廊道或过道，这又加强了土楼的通风性能。

Vertical-grid Window of Chengqi Tower

The vertical-grid window (a window with patterns of vertical grids) is a type of window commonly used in ancient times. It is relatively simple in design. The windows of round clay buildings are generally vertical-grid windows. They provide excellent ventilation. Furthermore, since the windows of round clay buildings are generally facing passages, corridors and hallways, they can further reinforce the ventilation performance of the buildings.

漏窗，俗称"花墙头"、"漏花窗"、"什锦窗"，多用在住宅、园林当中。窗框的制作材料有石、砖、木三种，通常是把砖瓦件镶嵌在墙面上，构成各种精巧的图案。漏窗装饰始于明代中期，《园冶》一书中列举了十几种精巧细致的漏窗，常见的有方、圆、六角、八角、扇形、菱形、花形、叶形等，窗内纹样有连钱、叠锭、鱼

The perforated window, commonly known as "flowery wall top", "perforated-pattern window" or "miscellaneous window", is generally used in residential houses as well as courtyards. The materials used for the frame of perforated windows include stones, bricks and wood. It is usually formed by inlaying bricks or tiles in the opening on the surface of the wall to create a variety of delicate patterns. The decoration of perforated windows began during the middle of the Ming Dynasty (1368-1644). In the book titled *Yuan Ye* (garden cultivating), more than a dozen exquisitely detailed perforated windows are cited. The most commonly seen shapes of perforated windows are squares, circles, hexagons, octagons, fans, rhombus, flowers, and leaves. The inlaid patterns inside the perforated window include connected

苏州怡园碧梧楼凤馆铜钱纹花窗
窗户借用铜钱的形式，不过将钱纹的圆形处理成了八角形。
Coin-patterned Perforated Window of the Phoenix Hall of the Biwu Building in Suzhou Yiyuan Garden
The window utilized the shape of a coin and changed the circular shape of the coin pattern to an octagonal one.

鳞、宫式、夔式、竹节、菱花、海棠等。各式各样的精美图案，虽是为装点风景而设计，但其本身也是一种风景。

coins, stacked ingots, fish scales, palace-style, *Kui* (one-legged mythical monster)-style, bamboo joints, rhombus, begonia and so on. The wide range of exquisite designs of perforated windows is meant to decorate the landscape, while itself is a scene too.

- **"万象更新"漏窗**

一头憨态可掬的大象，身上的披巾刻着一盆万年青，寓意万象更新。大象周围饰有飘带，周围的棂格中还刻着葫芦、飘带纹。

Perforated Window with the Pattern of "All Is Renewed in Freshness"

An elephant in a drape inscribed with a pot of evergreen with the logo "All Is Renewed in Freshness". The elephant is surrounded by decorative ribbons and the surrounding grid structure is carved with the patterns of gourds and ribbon.

- **狮子林琴棋书画花窗**

琴棋书画图案与窗巧妙地结合在一起，镂空雕刻的图案造型别致。

Perforated Window with the Pattern of Zither, Chess, Calligraphy and Painting in the Lion Grove Garden

The images of lute, chess, calligraphy and painting are cleverly integrated into the window, with the hollowed-out patterns in delicate styles.

> 斗拱

斗拱，是中国传统建筑特有的构件，置于柱头和额枋、屋顶之间，其作用是加大房檐，传递屋顶负荷，减少跨度。中国重要传统建筑如宫殿、坛庙、寺观以及大式楼台、亭阁等都使用斗拱。斗拱的层

• 北京先农坛太岁殿镏金斗拱
Gold-gilded Brackets Used in the Taisui Hall of the Temple of Agriculture in Beijing

> The Wood Bracket

The wood bracket is a unique component used in traditional Chinese architectures. Placed between top of columns and architraves and the roofing, it can extend the eave, distribute the load of the rooftops and reduce the horizontal span. Such important Chinese traditional architecture as palaces, altars, temples, shrines and large-scale towers, platform, gazebo and pavilions make extensive use of wood brackets. The more layers of structure the bracket extends, the higher class the architecture is. Prior to the Ming Dynasty (1368-1644), the wood bracket used to be the structural components that bore load and acted as decoration at the same time. After the Ming Dynasty, the load-bearing function of brackets began to weaken, while its role as a decoration began to materialize. By the time of

数越多，建筑的等级就越高。明朝以前，斗拱是有承重作用的结构件，同时也有装饰作用。明代以后，斗拱的承重作用逐渐减弱，装饰性加强，至清代时，基本上已是装饰件。其构造精巧，造型美观，如盆景，似花篮。斗拱不仅结构精巧，而且表面装饰有彩绘图案，十分优美。

the Qing Dynasty (1644-1911), wood brackets were essentially decorative items. With compact structure and delicate form, wood brackets are attractive in appearance like a bonsai or a flower basket. It is not just compact in structure but elegant, with the surface decorated with beautiful painted designs.

● 五踩斗拱
Five-step Bracket

> 柱

　　柱是房屋大木结构中的承重构件，竖立安装在台基的柱顶石上。柱子一般是圆柱体，也有四方、海棠式、六方、八方等异形柱，但用途都相同。柱子下端插入柱础中，上端与枋木相连，形成稳定的结构。柱子因安装位置不同而有专名，如檐柱、金柱等。

　　中国古建筑的木构架结构是由大木作开始施工的。在台基建好后就要安装立柱。柱子是承托屋顶的主要构件，柱子的高矮决定了建筑物房间的高度，柱子的位置决定了房屋开间和进深的大小。每根柱子的下端都有柱顶石，柱子的上端与枋木和随梁枋用榫卯结构相连。柱子多以油漆、彩绘的方式进行装饰，例如宫殿、寺庙、民居的柱子

> The Pillar

The pillar is a load-bearing component of a building's large wooden structure, generally erected above the column base stone of the stylobate. Pillars are typically cylindrical in shape but may also be square, hexagonal, octagonal or begonia-shaped. Whatever shape it takes, its function remains the same. The bottom of the pillar is inserted into the column base and the top is connected to the square horizontal wood on top of pillars to constitute a stable structure. Pillars installed in different positions are differently named, such as the eave columns and the in-house columns.

The wood frame structures of Chinese ancient architecture were built from large timber. Once the stylobate is constructed, pillars are installed and serve as the main components to support the

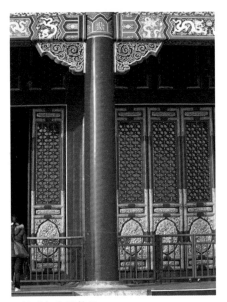

● 漆成红色的柱子
The Pillars of the Painted Red

roof. The length of the pillars determines the height of the rooms in the structure, while the positions of the pillars dictate the size and depth of the rooms. Every pillar has a pedestal boulder under its lower end, and its upper end is connected to the square horizontal wood on top of pillars and the horizontal beam accompanying the roof beam through tenons. Pillars are often decorated with oil or colored painting. For instance, pillars in palaces, temples and houses are generally painted red to express both festivity and dignity; pillars in the Hall of the Supreme Harmony of the Imperial Palace are painted in gold as symbolic of the highest rank and those in courtyards, corridors and pavilions are typically painted green to echo the surrounding scenery.

常漆成红色，喜庆而庄重；皇宫太和殿的柱子则被漆成金色，以显尊贵；园林亭廊的柱子多被漆成绿色，以呼应周围景色，等等。

楹联

楹联是指挂在楹（楹是指厅堂前面的柱子）上的对联。一般用木板、竹片做成弧形，在其上雕刻对联文字，之后再敷上红、绿、蓝、金或白色，加以精致装潢，悬挂于楹柱上。楹联是文学和书法的结合，符合中华民族的审美习惯，成为传统建筑常用的装饰手段，在园林中运用较广，既是点景手法，也是园林欣赏的重要内容。另外，还有一些形制特殊的楹联，更具装饰美感。

Column Couplets

Column couplets refer to the couplets that are written on scrolls and hung on the pillars in front of a hall. Column couplets are typically made of wooden or bamboo arc-shaped boards, with written couplets carved and colored in red, green, blue, gold or white on the surface of the boards. They hung on the pillars in front of a hall after being well decorated. The column couplets are a combination of literature and calligraphy in line with the aesthetic custom of Chinese people. It is a decorative method frequently used in traditional architecture and widely seen in courtyards. It is a means to decorate the landscape scene, as well as an important content in the appreciation of a garden. In addition, there are also some specially-shaped column couplets which claim more decorative beauty.

• 蕉叶联

把对联做成芭蕉叶的形状，就叫"蕉叶联"。这种形状优美别致的对联，多见于南方私家园林中，常挂于轩、榭、亭、阁的角落处。

Banana Leaf Couplet

When the couplet is made into the shape of a banana leaf, it is called a banana leaf couplet. This type of beautifully and uniquely shaped couplet is commonly seen in the private gardens in the south, hung on the corner of a loft, kiosk, gazebo or pavilion.

• 古琴联

做成古琴形状的木对联，叫"古琴联"。它是中国古建装饰追求雅韵情怀的表现。

Guqin Couplet

The wooden couplet made into the shape of a *Guqin* (ancient Chinese lute) is called a *Guqin* couplet, which represents the pursuit of music-related elegance and charm in ancient Chinese architectural decorations.

• 此君联

即竹节对联，将粗大的竹筒一剖两半，经打磨后在凸面上刻写对联，悬挂于园林、亭榭、书斋等处的室内或室外。这种竹制对联，做工很精细，装饰性很强，备受文人雅士喜爱。因竹子素有"君子"之誉，故称竹制对联为"此君联"。

Gentleman Couplet

It is namely a couplet on bamboo sections. A thick bamboo tube is split in half, polished, inscribed with couplet texts on its convex side and hung either indoors or outdoors in a garden, pavilion or study. This type of bamboo couplet is sophisticatedly crafted, highly decorative and widely favored by literati because bamboo is generally used figuratively as a gentleman (*Jun Zi* in Chinese). For this reason, the bamboo couplet is also called "*Jun*" couplet.

雕花石檐柱以龙纹为饰的，叫"龙柱"，一般用于外檐下，为外檐柱。其优点是不怕雨水，又非常精美，起到美化建筑的装饰性作用。石柱的形状有方形、圆形、槽形几种。清代寺观的山门、正殿的檐柱绝大多数是石雕龙柱，龙首有向上与向下之分。若一柱雕两条龙，便叫"雌雄蟠龙"；若龙首一

The eave column made of stone and decorated with dragon-patterned carvings is called a "dragon column", which is generally placed on the outside of the eave as an outer eave column. It has the advantage of being rain-resistant. Being exquisitely beautiful, it serves the decorative function of beautifying a building. The stone column is shaped in square, circular or grooved form. Vast majority of the eave columns used for the front gates and grand halls of temples in the Qing Dynasty (1644-1911) were stone dragon columns. The dragon head may be either faced upward or downward. If one single pillar has the carvings of two dragons, it is then called a column of "male and female curled-up dragons". Furthermore, if one of the dragons is facing upward while the other is facing downward, it is then called "heaven turning and earth shattering".

• 山东曲阜孔庙大成殿雕花石檐柱
Carved Stone Eave Column of the Dacheng Hall in the Confucius Temple, Located in Qufu, Shandong Province

向上一向下，便叫"翻天覆地"。龙柱上常配以云纹、水纹或虾蟹等水族动物。

以花鸟为饰的石檐柱，叫"花鸟柱"，多见于福建闽南地区。其多为方形石柱，常见者有百鸟朝凤柱和百鸟朝梅柱两种。百鸟朝凤柱纹样为石柱上下两端各有一只凤凰，并配以繁茂的牡丹花与叶和各式各样的鸟。百鸟朝梅柱纹样为一株粗壮的腊梅盘绕于柱上，千姿百

Dragon columns are frequently coupled with cloud patterns, water patterns and patterns of aquatic creatures such as crabs or prawns.

Stone eave columns decorated with flowers and birds are called "flower and bird column". They are frequently seen in the southern region of Fujian Province. They are usually square pillars. The two most common flower and bird columns are the those of "100 birds paying tributes to the phoenix" and that of "100 birds paying tributes to the plum". The pattern of the "100 birds paying tributes to the phoenix" includes two phoenixes on the top and at the bottom of the pillar, coupled with lush peony, peony leaves

● **山西王家大院一路连科木雕**

垂花门柱头上的木雕图案，充分利用垂花柱有限的空间，雕刻出一路连科图案，造型别致，堪称经典。寓意求取功名的考生可以顺利通过考试，金榜题名。

Wood Carving of "Heron and Lotus Path" with Implied Wish for Success in the Government's Exams All along, at the Wang's Compound in Shanxi Province

The wood carving on the pillar tops of the festooned door shows the full use of the limited space on the flower-hanging post to carve the pattern of heron and lotus path in such a delicate style. It is truly a classic masterpiece. The pattern implies the wish that a candidate striving for fame will pass the imperial examinations.

态的鸟栖息于树枝上，十分精美。

在垂花门麻叶梁头之下有一对倒悬的短柱，柱头向下，酷似一对含苞待放的花蕾，这种短柱称为"垂花柱"。顾名思义，垂花柱的雕饰十分精美，是垂花门装饰的重要组成部分。

柱础，是中国传统建筑构件的一种，俗称"柱顶石"。放置于柱子与台基之间，既可以防潮，又可分担柱子的承压力。柱础形式

● 山西平遥建筑中的雕狮柱础
Lion Column Base of a Building Located in Pingyao, Shanxi Province

and a multitude of various birds. The pattern of the "100 birds paying tributes to the plum" comprises a thick branch of blooming plum coiling around the pillar, with a variety of birds perching on tree twigs. It is truly delicate and beautiful.

Under the Ma-leave beam head of a festooned door, there is a pair of short upside-down pillars, making the head look like a pair of budding flowers. This pair of short pillars is called "hanging flower columns". As its name implies, the delicately sculpted hanging flower columns is an essential component to the decoration of a festooned door.

The column base is a building component of ancient Chinese architecture, more commonly known as "column top stone". Placed between the pillar and the stylobate, it is moisture-proof and can share the pressure bore by the pillar. There are two types of column bases. One is the single-layered column base, which may take the form of a drum, a basin, floor-paving lotus flowers and animals. The other is the multi-layered one made of two or more overlapping single-layered column bases in different forms.

有两大类，一类是单层式柱础，有鼓式、覆盆式、铺地莲花式、兽式等；另一类是多层式柱础，是由两种以上不同形式的单层式柱础重叠而成。

古代柱础上的雕刻，有铺地莲花式、仰覆莲花式、覆盆莲花式、海石榴花式、游龙戏水式、宝莲花式、牡丹花式等。其表面雕刻的内容题材更为广泛，包括花鸟、山水、图腾、历史故事、神话等。

The carvings on ancient column base may take the forms of floor-paving lotus flowers, the upward-facing and downward-facing lotus flowers, the downward-facing lotus flowers, the ocean pomegranate flowers, the water-plunging playful dragons, the treasure lotus flowers, and the peony flowers. The contents of the surface carvings are even more extensive, including flowers and birds, landscapes, totems, historical tales and myths.

• 北京圆明园遗址公园中的柱础，雕花十分精美
Beautifully-carved Column Base at the Relics of the Park in the Old Summer Palace of Beijing

● 梯形柱础
Trapezoid Column Base

● 如意柱础
Ruyi Column Base

● 卷草重层柱础
Multi-layered Coiled Grass Column Base

● 云凤柱础
Cloud-and-phoenix Column Base

雀替的制作材料由该建筑所用的主要建材决定，如木建筑上用木雀替，石建筑上用石雀替。雀替在北魏期间已具雏形，明清以来，雀替的雕刻装饰效果日渐突出，有龙、凤、仙鹤、花鸟、花篮、

The materials used in the production of the sparrow brace are decided by the primary construction materials used to build the architecture. For instance, a wooden sparrow brace would be used for a wood architecture and a stone sparrow brace would be used for a stone

中国建筑装饰
Chinese Architectural Decoration

金蟾等形式，雕法则有圆雕、浮雕、透雕。

牛腿的基本形状犹如上大下小的直角三角形，但也有少量是方形的。它依附在檐柱外向的上端，其上方直接或间接地承载着屋檐的重量。牛腿上的图案装饰十分丰富，且寓意深刻，包括动物题材、人类题材、山水题材等等。例如，牛腿上常雕刻狮子图案，古人认为狮子是瑞兽，可以镇宅驱邪、求得平

architecture. The sparrow brace was in its infancy during the Northern Wei Period (386-534). Its decorative effect became increasingly prominent since the Ming and Qing Dynasties (1368-1911). Some of the forms used for a sparrow brace include the dragon, phoenix, crane, flower and bird, flower basket and toad. Some of the sculpture methods include circular carving, relief carving and hollowed-out carving.

The basic shape of the corbel is a

● 精致的彩色雕花雀替
Exquisitely Carved and Colored Sparrow Brace

● 清代东阳木雕九狮纹牛腿 (图片提供：FOTOE)
Dongyang Wood Carving of the Nine-lion Pattern on the Corbel in the Qing Dynasty (1644-1911)

安。福禄寿三星、渔樵耕读等也常出现在牛腿上，此外还有山水画，梅兰竹菊、松柏石榴、莲荷牡丹等。

right-angled triangle with a wide top and narrow bottom. There are also a few of them in the shape of a square. It is attached to the upper and outer end of the eave column to directly or indirectly carry the weight of the eave above it. The corbel is rich in decorative patterns with meaningful themes such as animals, people or landscapes. For example, sometimes the corbel is carved with a lion on its surface. Since people in ancient times believed that lions were auspicious animals, these carvings were intended to ward off evil spirits and express hope for peace. Patterns of the "three stars of happiness, fortune, and longevity" and "lives of fishery, logging, farming, and studying" also frequently appear on corbels. There are also patterns of landscape painting with meandering mountain ranges, as well as "plum blossom, orchid, bamboo and chrysanthemum", "pine trees, furs and pomegranate" and "lotus and peony flowers".

> 梁枋

梁，是屋顶木构架中横向负重的构件之一，也可称其为"桄"。中国传统建筑以土木结构为主，梁是建筑必不可少的构造，根据部位的不同，梁有很多专用名称。例如，攒尖式屋顶的木架构中，不直接交会在立柱上，用于加高和收缩

> The Roof Beam

The beam, also known as the "girder", is one of the horizontal weight-bearing components in the wood framework of the roof. Traditional Chinese architecture was dominated by wood and earth structures and the beam was an indispensable structure. The beam has various specific names in accordance

● 北京颐和园里的抹角梁
Blunt-corner Beam at the Summer Palace in Beijing

屋顶的梁叫做"抹角梁"。梁不仅仅起到房屋的支架的实用功能，也具有极强的美化装饰功能。传统建筑中的梁常被彩绘上各种精美的图案，既可以防止梁受潮变形，又是一种精美的点缀。

枋是安装在两柱之间或两柱上端的扁方形木材，通过榫卯将两个柱子的上端连在一起。有斗拱的建筑，要专设几根枋，用来承托、拉拽、压住斗拱。枋也安装在檩（檩，又叫"桁"、"栋"，架设在枋木之上，或架于前后斗拱之

• **穿插枋**

穿插枋用于抱头梁或挑尖梁的下面。作用是承托抱头梁或挑尖梁，加强抱头梁或挑尖梁的承重能力。

Interjecting *Fang*

The interjecting *Fang* is used underneath the head-embracing beam or the tapering beam to support them and strengthen their load-bearing capacity.

with where it is positioned. For example, in the wood structure of a pyramidal roof, the beam is not directly placed on the top of pillars. Those used to raise the height of the roof and taper off the top of the roof are called "blunt-corner beam". Beams have not only the practical function of supporting houses, but also highly decorative functions. In traditional architectures, beams are often painted with a variety of beautiful patterns in order to prevent deformation caused by dampness and to provide exquisite embellishment.

The *Fang* is a flat square timber installed horizontally between two pillars or on the top of two pillars. Through the use of tenons, the *Fang* is connected with the top of two pillars. Those buildings with wood brackets require specifically designed *Fang* to support, pull or press the wood bracket. *Fang* can also be installed below the ridgepole (also known as the "purlin", is mounted above the *Fang* wood or in between the front and back bracket set) and beam to strengthen the load-bearing capacity of ridgepoles and beams and prevent their deformation. *Fang* is given different names according to the specific locations they are installed.

间）和梁的下面，有加强檩和梁的承重能力，防止檩和梁变形的作用。枋木，因安装位置不同而有专名。中国传统建筑以木构架为主，枋是屋顶的重要支撑部分，同时也是彩画装饰的重点部位。

Traditional Chinese architectures are primarily built of wooden structures, and the *Fang* is not only an important supporting part of the roof, but also a key part for color-painted decorations.

- **脊枋**

脊枋即脊柱之下的方形木材，位于屋架的最高处，其上便是脊檩。脊枋的作用是承托脊檩，加强脊檩的承重能力。

Ridge *Fang*

The square timber under the spine pillar and on the highest part of the roof frame is called the ridge *Fang*. The ridge *Fang* is used to support and strengthen the load-bearing capacity of the ridge purlin.

- **挑尖梁和抱头梁**

在檐头部位的梁，一种是抱头梁，另一种是挑尖梁。

Tapering Beam and Head-embracing Beam

The tapering beam and the head-embracing beam are the exposed portion of the beam at the end of the eaves.

- 大、小额枋

额枋指檐柱之间的方形木材。有的建筑会用两根额枋，通常上面的一根稍大，叫"大额枋"；下面的一根较小，叫"小额枋"。

Big and Small Architraves

The architrave refers to the square piece of wood between eave columns. Some buildings make use of two architraves. The slightly larger one on top is called the "large architrave" while the slightly smaller piece below is called the "small architrave".

- 坐斗枋

坐斗枋是位于大额枋之上的一条方木，用于承托斗拱，斗拱最底下的大斗就"坐"于平板枋上，故叫"坐斗枋"。

Bracket-seat *Fang*

The bracket-seat *Fang* is a piece of square wood located above the large architrave to support the wood bracket, and the big bracket at the bottom sits directly on this flat panel of *Fang*, called the "bracket-seat *Fang*".

> 护栏

　　栏杆有木栏杆、石栏杆、石木栏杆、矮墙等种类，安装在高台、台基的边缘，或装于两柱之间，窗下，以代替半墙，多见于临水建筑、楼阁、走廊等处。

　　木栏杆，多用于临水建筑、楼阁、走廊等处。竖木为栏，横木

> The Guard Rail

The railing comes in various forms, such as the wood railing, the stone railing, the wood and stone railing, low walls and so on. It is installed on the border of tall decks and stylobates, in between pillars, or beneath windows as a replacement for low walls. It is commonly seen on those buildings near waterfronts, as well as

● 花式栏杆

花式栏杆是寻杖栏杆的变形和简化。花式栏杆通常不用寻杖，而是在整个栏杆板上雕刻各种纹样，有冰裂纹、盘长纹、龟背锦等。用料较轻巧，花式变化丰富，样式别致。

Flower-patterned Railings

The flower-patterned railings are a simplified variation of the wood staff railing. The flower-patterned railing generally does not utilize a staff, but the railing boards are carved with a variety of patterns instead, such as ice-crack patterns, Buddhist lucky patterns and turtle-back brocade patterns. The materials utilized for flower-patterned railings are light with various patterns and unique styles.

为杆，为防护而设，装于两柱之间或窗下，以代替半墙。木栏杆有高低两种，较高的多为寻杖栏杆、靠背栏杆（也称"美人靠"、"吴王靠"），此外还有花式栏杆和瓶式栏杆。

- 寻杖木栏杆

寻杖木栏杆是最常见的一种，多用于檐下栏杆和楼梯两侧扶手。其主要部件有望柱、寻杖、扶手、腰枋、下枋、地栿、绦环板、牙子以及荷叶净瓶等。

Wood Staff Railing

The wood staff railing is the most commonly seen railing used as handrails underneath the eaves or on both sides of a staircase. Its main components include the baluster, the handrails, the waist *Fang*, the lower *Fang*, the ground rail, the relief-line board, the teeth, and the lotus-leaf vase, etc.

pavilions and corridors.

Wood railing is generally used on buildings near waterfronts, as well as pavilions and corridors. The vertical wood pieces are called *Lan*, and the horizontal pieces are called *Gan*. It is a protection design installed between two pillars or beneath windows as a replacement for half walls. There are two kinds of wood railings: the tall one and the low one. Most of the taller railings are staff railings (*Xun Zhang* railings), backrest railings (*Kao Bei* railings), also known as the "beauty backrest" or "King Wu's backrest", the flower-patterned railings and the vase-shaped railings.

- 靠背栏杆

靠背栏杆又名"吴王靠"、"美人靠"、"飞来椅",是一种有椅子靠背的栏杆,高度在50厘米左右,长度依所属建筑开间的尺寸而定。常用在园林的亭、榭、轩、阁等小型建筑的外围,即可做栏杆,亦可供人休息,安全舒适。

Backrest Railings

The backrest railing, also known as the "King Wu's backrest", "beauty backrest" or "the chair flew from afar", is a type of railing with a chair's back for backrest. It is approximately 50 centimeters in height, with the length set relative to the span of the construction. It is frequently seen in the outer rings of lofts, kiosks, gazebos, pavilions and other small structures in the garden. It not only serves as a railing but also provide people with a place to rest safely and comfortably.

- 瓶式木栏杆

瓶式栏杆是清代受到外国建筑影响而出现的一种西洋式栏杆。栏板采用由多根木料旋成的瓶式直棂条,而不是栏板形式。瓶式栏杆经过匠人的彩绘,装饰性更强。

Vase-shaped Wood Railing

The vase-shaped railing is a type of Western-styled railing under the influence of foreign architecture in the Qing Dynasty (1644-1911). The rail board is made of multiple vase-shaped vertical bars by cutting the wood materials, instead of the traditional rail board. Color-painted by craftsmen, the vase-shaped railing becomes more decorative in its attributes.

石栏杆又叫"勾栏"，用于殿堂、亭榭、月台的须弥座台式高台或台基上，也用于石桥、华表、碑、园中水岸边，其用途是维护安全。装饰性极好，又有分隔、或连接不同景区的作用，能够丰富园林的空间层次感。

Stone railings, also known as "*Gou Lan*" in Chinese, are used as safety precaution on the high-raised platform or stylobate with the Buddhist Sumera seat as seen in palace halls, pavilions and moon platforms as well as on stone bridges, ornamental columns, monuments and banks of water in gardens. However, since stone railings have excellent decorative effects and can separate or connect different scenic spots, they are often used to enrich the layered space and sense of depth in the courtyard.

● 北京恭王府花园石栏杆
石栏杆由许多组小单元组成，每组包括地伏、栏板、望柱，起头或收尾处再加抱鼓石。
Stone Railing in the Flower Garden of Beijing's Prince Gong's Mansion
The stone railings are composed of numerous small units. Every unit includes such elements as ground rail, rail board and baluster, with drum-holding stones at the beginning and the end of the railings.

望柱

望柱也称"栏杆柱",是位于栏杆的栏板和栏板之间的短柱。望柱分柱头与柱身,柱头部分有很多雕刻性装饰,常见于宫殿、园林、桥梁等建筑中。

Baluster

The baluster, also known as the "railing baluster", is a short pillar located between railing boards. A baluster is composed of a baluster head and a baluster body. The baluster head is usually carved with numerous decorations, as seen so commonly in the architecture of palaces, courtyards, bridges and so forth.

- **石望柱**
Stone Baluster

- **铜望柱**
Copper Baluster

石望柱的柱头因装饰纹样不同而有很多种，使用必须符合规定，其官式做法有口龙柱头、蕉叶柱头、云龙柱头、凤柱头、狮子柱头、八不蹭柱头、莲瓣柱头、覆莲柱头、石榴柱头、二十四节气柱头、风云柱头、仙人柱头、叠落云子柱头、马尾柱头等多种形式。民间的石望柱柱头的纹样则比较随意。

Since the baluster head of a stone baluster can be decorated with various patterns, its usage must comply with the regulations. The typical baluster head designated for official usage include the dragon mouth baluster head, banana leaf baluster head, cloud dragon baluster head, phoenix baluster head, lion baluster head, eight no-rubbings baluster head, lotus-petal baluster head, inverted lotus

• 北京北海的石榴望柱头
Pomegranate Baluster Head in Beihai, Beijing

• 北京北海琼岛莲花望柱头
Lotus Baluster Head on Qiong Island, Beihai, Beijing

baluster head, pomegranate baluster head, twenty-four solar terms baluster head, wind and cloud baluster head, the immortal baluster head, cascading cloud baluster head, horse tail baluster head and so forth. In contrast, the stone baluster in the civilian context has more free usage of the patterns for baluster head.

- 北京北海琼岛延楼长廊云龙纹望柱头

云龙纹望柱头因柱头上装饰云龙纹而得名。工匠们充分利用柱头有限的空间，用祥云衬托龙的威势。龙身周围饰以云纹。龙纹浮雕，龙身上的鳞纹清晰可见。

Cloud Dragon Baluster Head of the Yanlou Tower Corridor, Located on Qiong Island in Beihai, Beijing

The cloud dragon baluster head got its name from its patterns of dragon and cloud on the baluster head decoration. The craftsmen fully utilized the limited space on the baluster head to depict the dragon and support its powerful stance by the usage of patterned cloud. The body of the dragon is also adorned with clouds. The dragon is embossed on the surface with its scale patterns clearly visible.

> 台基

　　台基是建筑的承台基座，包含房屋的基础、柱顶石等。中国传统建筑很重视台基，把台基、墙体、屋顶视为建筑的三大组成部

· 北京故宫太和门石狮座下的须弥座
Buddhist Sumeru Base under the Stone Lions of the Gate of the Supreme Harmony in the Forbidden City, Beijing

> The Stylobate

The stylobate serves as the foundation base of a building, and contains the groundwork, column base and others. Traditional Chinese architecture attaches great importance to the stylobate, and considered the stylobate, the wall and the roof as the three major components of a building. Stylobates are divided into the basic stylobate and the sumeru stylobate. Moon platform and balustrades are also important components of a stylobate.

　　Stylobates may differ in accordance with the rank of their respective architecture. In ancient times, officials had strict regulations and rules as to the use of stylobates. According to the *Qing Dynasty Records (Da Qing Hui Dian)*, houses that belong to the officials of the level below a prince but above Level Three in rank should have the standard

• 龙头须弥座

此须弥座带有石栏，并在望柱
之下、须弥座的上枋部位，安
装了一排石雕龙头，位于角部
的龙头较大，为爬出状，龙头
嘴部有一个排水孔，可排泄须
弥座台面上的雨水。

Dragon Head Buddhist Sumeru
Base

A row of stone dragon heads is
set on the upper *Fang* under the
baluster, surrounded by stone
railings. The dragon heads located
at the corners are larger in size
and posed in a crawling form. A
drain hole is located at the back of
the dragon's mouth, which serves
to drain the rainwater from the
Buddhist Sumeru base.

分。台基分为普通台基和须弥座
式台基，月台与栏杆也是台基的
重要组成部分。

　台基因建筑物的级别而有所不
同。古代官方对台基的使用有严格
的规定，据《大清会典》记载：公
侯以下，三品官以上的房屋台基准
高二尺；四品官以下到市民的房屋
台基高一尺。

　佛教中的圣山名"须弥山"，
把须弥山作为佛像的基座象征着
佛坐在圣山上，其形象更加神圣崇
高，中国传统建筑中额台基地广
泛运用须弥座。须弥座的体积虽
有大小，但基本形态是相同的。

stylobate at two *Chi* (two-thirds of a
meter) high. Houses that belong to Level-
Four officials and downward to civilians
should have the standard stylobate at one
Chi (one-third of a meter) high.

　To make the sacred mountain in
Buddhism, the Sumeru Mountain, into
the base for the statue of Buddha is to
signify the holiness and loftiness of
Buddha sitting on the holy mountain.
Known as the Buddhist Sumeru base,
the base is considered to be sacred and
noble, and thus has been widely used
as the stylobate in traditional Chinese
architecture. Although they may vary in
size, Buddhist Sumeru bases are identical
in shape. The various parts of the

须弥座从上到下的各部分分别为上枋、上枭、束腰、下枭、下枋和圭脚等。

Buddhist Sumeru base are categorized from top to bottom into upper *Fang*, upper cyma, waist, lower cyma, lower *Fang* and foot.

● 束腰处有椀花结带纹的须弥座

因汉白玉须弥座要用于不同等级的建筑，故对汉白玉须弥座的雕花处理也不同，最简单的一种是仅在束腰部位进行椀花雕刻，其余各处均无雕花。椀花结带纹，是一种上下对称的纹样，动感很强。

Pattern of Splashing Tea Foam with Ribbon Band on the Waist of the Buddhist Sumeru Base

Since the white marble Buddhist Sumeru base are used in architecture of different classes, the carving patterns used for white marble Buddhist Sumeru base are also differently handled. The simplest pattern is the use of splashing tea foam pattern carvings on the waist portion of the Buddhist Sumeru base, while the remaining portions are kept in plain surface. The pattern of splashing tea foam with ribbon band is vertically symmetrical which shows a very strong dynamic sense.

● 须弥座四角位置上的喷水兽

喷水兽的实际作用是排水，它是一种龙形兽身的瑞兽，因大部只做出头部，又叫螭首。位于须弥座四角位置上的瑞兽，形体较大，露出身体的一半，形象也很生动，叫大龙头或四角龙头。其他部位的龙头都较小，叫小龙头或正身龙头。

Water-sprinkling Beasts at the Four Corners of the Buddhist Sumeru Base

The water-sprinkling beast is practically used as a water outlet. It is an auspicious animal in the shape of a dragon with the body of a beast. Since usually only its head is exposed outside, it is also called "*Chi Shou*" (the head of a hornless dragon). The water-sprinkling beasts at the four corners of the Buddhist Sumeru base are larger in size, with only half of their bodies exposed in vivid forms. They are called the large dragon head or four-corner dragon head. The dragon heads on the other parts of the Buddhist Sumeru base are smaller in size and called the small dragon head or full-front dragon head.

• 束腰和上枋处有雕花的须弥座

这种汉白玉须弥座的雕饰较多，一般出现在束腰和上枋上。束腰部位仍是椀花结带纹，上枋上雕刻有卷草纹。

Buddhist Sumeru Base with Carvings on Its Waist and Upper *Fang* Section

This type of white marble Buddhist Sumeru base generally has more carvings on its waist and upper *Fang* sections. The carving on the waist is the pattern of splashing tea foam with ribbon band while the carving on the upper *Fang* section is the curled grass pattern.

• 全雕花的须弥座

这种汉白玉须弥座的所有部位上都有雕花。束腰部位仍是椀花结带纹，上、下枋多雕刻卷草纹、宝相花纹或云龙纹，上、下枭多雕刻莲花瓣纹。

Fully-carved Buddhist Sumeru Base

This type of Buddhist Sumeru base is fully carved throughout its bodies. The pattern of splashing tea foam with ribbon is still used on its waist, while the curled grass, Baoxiang flowers and cloud and dragon patterns are used on its upper *Fang* and lower *Fang* sections. Its upper cyma and lower cyma are often carved with lotus-petal patterns.

> 铺地

　　传统建筑装饰中对地面的装饰手法主要为铺地。铺地就是通过镶嵌、拼接的方法构成各种各样的花纹、图案，增添地面的视觉效果。

　　铺地，又叫墁地，指用砖石铺

• 散水
Apron

> The Ground Paving

The floors in traditional architecture are primarily decorated through the use of ground paving techniques, where various types of patterns and pictures are inlaid or pieced up together to increase the visual effect of the ground.

　　Also known as "*Man Di*", ground paving refers to the brick or stone pavement on the indoor or outdoor ground, including the roads in the courtyard and gardens. Indoor ground paving refers to the pavement on the indoor ground where square bricks or long bricks are generally used. There are three kinds of courtyard ground paving: apron, paved path in courtyards or gardens and paved square. Among the three, paved path in courtyards or gardens involves more varieties of skills. Apron is the brick pavement made on the

- **长砖墁地砖缝**

用砖墁地，会因砖的排列方式不同而有不同的缝隙，即"砖缝"。砖缝其实是一类图案，常见的有十字缝、拐子锦、褥子面、人字缝、丹墀、套八方等。

Brick Gaps of Long-brick Paved Square

In bricked paved square, different gaps may form as result of the various ways of arranging the bricks. These gaps are called brick gaps. In fact, brick gaps are also a type of pattern. Some of the frequently seen brick gaps include the cross gaps, brocade of cane gaps, quilt surface gaps, "人" character gaps, red palace-steps gaps and eight-direction joint gaps.

- **海墁**
Paved Square

设室内外的地面，也包括庭院和园林中的道路。室内墁地，指建筑内部地面的铺装，一般用方砖或长砖墁地。庭院墁地有散水、甬路、海墁三类，其中，甬路的做法较多。散水是在屋檐下、台阶旁，沿着前、后檐及山墙在地面上墁砖。墁砖要略有坡度，让屋檐下的雨水尽快流走，房屋四周没有积水，这样

ground along the front eave, back eave, and gables beneath the eaves or beside the stairs. Brick pavement is slightly sloped to facilitate the flow of rainwater so that no stagnant water will be accumulated around the building. It not only protects the groundwork from water erosion, but also beautifies the ground around the building. The frequently used apron includes the patterns of first-grade

● 雕花甬路

雕花甬路主要是指在甬路两侧铺散水的位置，改用有雕花的方砖，或用瓦片组成好看的纹饰，也可采用多色卵石摆成图案。

Paved Path in Courtyards or Gardens with Carved Patterns

Paved path in courtyards or gardens with carved patterns refers to the apron area on both sides of the paved path in courtyards or gardens being replaced by pattern-carved square bricks or attractive patterns of pieced-up tiles. Sometimes, multi-colored pebbles are also used to create patterns.

便可以保护地基不受雨水的侵蚀，也有美化建筑周围地面的作用。常用的散水，有一品书、连环锦等铺法。另外，甬路、御路的两侧也要有散水。甬路是庭院中的主要交通线，一般用方砖或长砖墁地。甬路分大式做法和小式做法。宫廷中的甬路，称为御路，采用条石墁地，两侧也要用砖铺设散水。海墁指在庭院中除散水、甬路之外，在其他

volume and serial brocade. Sometimes, apron is also used on both sides of paved path in courtyards or gardens and the imperial paths. Paved path in courtyards or gardens is the main traffic route in a courtyard. It is usually paved out of square bricks or long bricks. Paved path in courtyards or gardens can be built in big-type or small-type approaches. The paved path in courtyards or gardens in palaces, paved with bar stones, is called

地方也都用条砖墁地的做法。"海墁"是老北京话，"海"是全部、没有边界之意。业内有"竖墁甬路横墁地"的口诀，是说海墁的条砖要沿东西方位放置。

花街铺地是园林铺地种类之一，多见于江南园林。花街铺地就是用砖、瓦、石片、印石、瓷缸片等材料铺成各种图案花纹的地面。它的种类很多，大多是就地取材，

● **方砖卵石嵌花路**

这是北方宫苑中常用铺地做法。一般是道路中间铺方砖，方砖两侧铺卵石带，用砖、瓦分段，将卵石拼成寿字、如意、铜钱、扇形、海棠等图案，再以各色卵石填心。

Patterned Road Inlaid with Square Bricks and Pebbles

This is a very common ground paving practice used in palaces and courtyards in the north. Square bricks are generally paved in the middle of the road, with pebbles paved along both sides. Brick and tile fragments are used to outline the pebbles in the forms of the Chinese character "寿" (longevity), *Ruyi*, coin, fan, begonia or others, Then pebbles of different colors are used to fill in the centers.

the imperial path. It also has apron installed on both sides. Paved square refers to the bar-brick-paved space in courtyards other than the apron and paved path areas. The paved square (*Hai Man* in Chinese) is an old Beijing term: "*Hai*" means all, or being without borders. In the industry, the mnemonic jargon "Paved path in courtyards or gardens in vertical directions and paved square in horizontal directions" refers to the fact that the bar bricks used for paved square should be laid in east and west orientation.

Flower-street ground paving is a type of garden ground paving frequently seen in gardens in southern China. It's the combined use of bricks, tiles, stone plates, pebble stones and ceramic fragments to create various types of pictures and patterns for the ground pavement. There are many kinds of flower-street ground paving, but most of them make use of local materials. The low-value materials may achieve high-class effects and accomplish high degrees of craftsmanship and artistry. For instance, a simple use of bricks and tiles may compose basket pattern, whorl pattern, chessboard pattern and "人" character pattern. The use of bricks can also form such frames as hexagons, hexagonal frames, hexagonal

低材高用，体现了较高的技艺水平。如有纯用砖瓦，摆成席纹、斗纹、间方纹、人字纹等；有以砖瓦做成六角、套六角、套六方、套八方等方框，在框内填充各色卵石或碎瓷片；亦可用卵石与瓦混砌，做成套钱、芝花等纹；还有用各色卵石铺地，花纹如织锦，色彩对比鲜明。

direction, and octagonal direction and fill the inside of the frame with a variety of colored pebbles and porcelain pieces. Furthermore, pebbles and tiles can also be mixed in use to form coin frame and flower patterns. Such ground paving as paved with colored pebbles may display patterns like brocade in a sharp contrast of colors.

• 苏州狮子林里八卦纹铺地，用于辟邪除灾，带来吉祥

Eight Diagrams-patterned Ground Paving in Suzhou Lion Grave Garden, Believed to Ward off Evil Spirits, Prevent Disasters and Bring in Good Luck

• 花街铺地之植物纹图案

Vegetation Pattern in Flower-street Ground Paving

• 吉祥如意铺地，双鱼的鱼鳞、尾巴雕刻突出，形象生动

Ground Paving Meaning Good Luck and Happiness, with the Scales and Tails of Two Fish Vividly Carved

室内铺地

建筑内部地面的铺装，一般用方砖或长砖墁地。从工艺上分细墁和糙墁两种。还有一种最高级的墁地方式叫"金砖墁地"，仅用于最高级别的宫廷大殿中。

细墁，一种高级的砖铺地面工艺，所用方砖经过砍打、细磨，仔细墁平后，要进行表处理，包括清理砖体表面、用磨头蘸水再次将砖体打磨平整，待干后再用生桐油反复擦拭。为防潮及减少起沙，一般都要铺设水磨方砖。

• 细墁铺地
Fine Ground Paving

粗墁，是一种砖铺地面工艺，所用砖未经过砍打、细磨处理，但墁砖时与细墁工艺相同，只是最后不抹油灰，也不用生桐油，只用白沙子灰勾缝。

金砖墁地，金砖是一种用澄浆泥烧制而成的大方砖，规格为50厘米×50厘米×8厘米，是专门为宫廷烧制的方砖。质地坚硬，表面有光泽，敲之有金属声，故称为"金砖"。

The Indoor Ground Paving

The indoor ground surface is generally paved with square bricks or long bricks. The indoor ground paving can be classified into the rough ground paving and fine ground paving by their respective craftsmanship. There is also a ground paving of the highest class, called the "gold brick ground paving", which is seen only in the hall of the highest-class imperial palaces.

Fine ground paving is a high-class type of brick pavement. The square bricks utilized in this ground paving are cut and sanded, then carefully leveled after being paved, and processed

粗墁铺地

Rough Ground Paving

on the surface by clearing and water milling the surface. They will then be polished and cleaned before they are repeatedly rubbed with raw tung oil after they are dried. The square bricks are often water milled in order to make them moisture-proof and less friable.

Rough ground paving is a type of brick ground paving that makes use of uncut, unpolished bricks, while the paving process is the same as the fine ground paving. However, the rough ground paving process does not wipe away excess putty, nor use raw tung oil at the end, but uses fine white sand to fill the joints between bricks.

The gold brick ground paving uses a type of large square brick made and fired from clear clay pulp. With a dimension of 50 cm * 50 cm * 8 cm, these square bricks are specifically produced for palaces. Since they are solid, hard, polished and sound like metal when struck, they are called "gold bricks".

北京故宫乾清宫内的金砖墁地

Gold Brick Paved Ground at the Palace of Heavenly Purity in the Forbidden City, Beijing

> 室外建筑的其他装饰

石碑

宫殿、寺观前常设有石碑，石碑是由碑首、碑身、碑座三部分组成。碑首，早期有圆首形和尖首形两种，这大约与周代琬圭和琰圭两种礼玉有关。碑身，是碑的主体部分，一般用竖长方形的巨石雕刻而成。碑的正面，叫"碑阳"，一般以刻文字为主，也有刻山水、人物、花草、禽鸟、地图等。碑的背面多刻有诸如门生、故吏和出资建碑者的姓名等文字，叫做"碑阴"。碑侧也刻有文字和精美的图案花纹。碑座，是安放碑身的石座，称为"趺"。早期的碑座为简单的长方形，四面各有朱雀、玄武、青龙、白虎四灵神。南北

> Other Decorations of Outdoor Architectures

The Stone Tablet

The stone tablet is usually set up in front of palaces and temples. A stone tablet is composed of the tablet head, the tablet body and the tablet base. The earlier tablet heads were circular or pointy in shape, which may have something to do with the two types of ritual jade, jade tablet with round head and jade tablet with pointed head, from the Zhou Dynasty (1046 B.C.-221 B.C.). The tablet body is the main part of a stone tablet, which is generally carved out of a vertical rectangular boulder. The front of the tablet, called "*Bei Yang*", is typically carved with texts and sometimes with landscapes, personages, flowers, birds, maps, or other items. The back of the tablet, also known as "*Bei Yin*", is often

石碑下的龟形兽为赑屃，是龙的九子之一，形状似乌龟，好负重，身上驮有石碑。在寺庙或祠堂建筑里，常能见到它。碑文两旁的文龙是负屃，它平生好文，所以多被用来装饰碑文两侧。

Stone Tablet in Front of the Qingyang Palace in Chengdu, Sichuan Province

The tortoise-like beast beneath the stone tablet is called "*Bi Xi*" in Chinese, one of the dragon's nine sons. It is tortoise-shaped and has a great load-bearing capacity. It has a stone tablet mounted on its back and is frequently seen inside temples and ancestral halls. The dragons on both sides of the inscription are called "*Fu Xi*". Since Fu Xi enjoyed literature, they are often used as decorations by the side of the inscriptions.

朝时期出现了龟形碑座，称为"龟跌"，将碑座改制成为龟形，是期望石碑保持永久之意。

铜铸饰品

宫殿、寺庙前常有龟形、鹤形、龙形等形象的铜铸饰品。摆放铜铸饰品既加强了建筑环境美观性，又是身份尊贵的象征。除此之外还有铜坐狮、铜凤、铜麒麟、铜象、铜牛等，除铜牛外，一般均以成对、成组方式陈设。

carved with the names of the followers, disciples or individual who funded the construction of the tablet. The sides of the tablet may also have carved texts and exquisite patterns. The tablet base, also known as the "*Fu*", is the stone base on which the tablet body is mounted. Earlier tablet base were made into simple rectangular shapes with the four spiritual creatures, red sparrow, dark turtle, green dragon and white tiger, carved on each of its four sides. The tortoise-shaped tablet base, called "*Gui Fu*", appeared during the Southern and Northern Dynasties (420-589), with the tablet bases essentially shaped like a tortoise. They

- 北京故宫太和殿前的铜鹤
Bronze Crane in Front of the Hall of Supreme
Harmony in the Forbidden City, Beijing

symbolized the permanence of the stone tablet.

The Cast Bronze Decoration

The front of palaces and temples is often decorated with bronze decorations cast in the form of tortoises, cranes, dragons and so on. Bronze decorations not only strengthen the aesthetic beauty in the environment of a building, but also symbolize its noble status. Beyond that, there are also bronze lions, phoenixes, kylins, elephants and bulls among other creatures. Aside from bronze bulls, most of these statues are generally displayed in pairs or sets.

- 乾清宫前的铜龟
Bronze Tortoise in Front of the Palace of Heavenly Purity

日晷

日晷是古代的时钟，晷盘面平行于赤道面，晷针垂直于晷盘面。它是利用太阳的投影和地球自转的原理，借指针所生阴影的位置来显示时刻。古代宫殿、园林等建筑空地处常放有日晷，方便人们知道时间。

The Sundial

The sundial was used to tell the time in ancient times. The surface of the sundial disk is parallel to the equatorial plane and the dial needle is set perpendicular to it. Using the principle of solar projection and the rotation of the earth, the shadow of the dial needle will display the time by the marked scale. The sundial used to be placed in the open space in front of such buildings as ancient palaces and courtyards to make it convenient for people to determine the time.

● 北京故宫太和殿前的日晷
Sundial in Front of the Hall of Supreme Harmony in the Forbidden City in Beijing

鼎式香炉

鼎式香炉也叫做香炉鼎，从古代一直沿用至今，可用来燃烧檀香和松枝，能辟邪，又能用来祈求吉祥。在周代有"天子九鼎，诸侯七鼎，卿大夫五鼎，元士三鼎"等使用数量的规定。

The Tripod Incense Burner

The tripod incense burner, also known as the incense burner tripod, has been used since ancient times. Burning sandalwood or pine log in the tripod incense burner can ward off evil influences and bring forth good luck. During the Zhou Dynasty (1046 B.C.-221 B.C.), the use of tripod vessels was regulated as, "Nine tripod vessels are used by the emperor, seven tripod vessels used by dukes and princes, five tripod vessels by patriarchal clans, and three tripod vessels by lower officials."

• 北京故宫太和殿鼎式香炉
Tripod Incense Burner at the Hall of Supreme Harmony in the Forbidden City in Beijing

传统建筑室内装饰
The Interior Decoration of Traditional Architecture

　　室内装饰是中国传统建筑装饰不可忽略的重要部分，讲究层次分明、有序、协调。传统建筑室内装饰包括挂落、门帘架、罩、天花、藻井等构件，这些构件的装饰功能与其结构功能几乎同样重要。受技艺、地域、民族、宗教等因素影响，传统建筑的室内装饰风格各有不同。

As an important part of Chinese traditional architecture that cannot be neglected, interior decoration puts much emphasis on structured layers, orderliness and coordination. The interior decoration of traditional architecture is mostly manifested in hanging fascia, door curtain frame, mask, ceiling patterns, caisson and other components. The decorative functions of these components are almost as equally important as their structural functions. Influenced by such factors as craftsmanship, geographic region, ethnicity, religion and so on, the interior decoration of traditional architecture varies in styles.

> 挂落

挂落，是额枋下的一种建筑构件，常用镂空的木板或雕花板做成，也可由细小的木条搭接而成，

> The Hanging Fascia

The hanging fascia is a construction component set below the architrave. It is usually either made of hollowed wooden frame or carved panels, or composed of small strips of wood for the purpose of dividing the interior space. More often than not, hanging fascia is the focus of the architectural decoration with openwork carving or colored treatment. The basic patterns of hanging fascia include steps of prospect, lantern frames,

• 乔家大院第六院敦品第大门挂落八骏图
Hanging Fascia with the Pattern of Eight Spirited Horses, Hung from the Gate of Dunpindi (House of Tempered Character), the Sixth Courtyard of Qiao's Compound

● 双凤朝阳木雕挂落
Wooden Hanging Fascia Carved with Patterns of Two Phoenixes Darting toward the Sun

用来划分室内空间。同时，挂落在建筑中常常做为装饰的重点，做透雕或彩绘处理。挂落主要有步步锦、灯笼框、冰裂纹、葵纹等纹样，还有许多琴棋书画、雅宅众宝纹、八骏图、双凤朝阳等吉祥图案，代表吉祥平安等美好愿望。

ice cracks, sunflowers and so forth. There are also such auspicious patterns as images of zither, chess, calligraphy and painting, patterns of elegant house with all the treasures, pictures of eight spirited horses, two phoenixes darting toward the sun, and so on, bearing such good wishes as good fortune and peace.

> 门帘架

门帘架常在明间（建筑正中的一间）隔扇的外面用来挂门帘，也有次间用门帘架。除了有挂门帘的实用作用之外，门帘架还有很强的装饰性，门帘架上常常雕刻各种图案。

> The Door Curtain Frame

The door curtain frame is often installed outside of the partition door of the room in the very center of the building to hang the door curtain. Sometimes it may also be seen in the side rooms. In addition to its practical function of hanging a curtain, the door curtain frame is also highly decorative and is often carved into a variety of patterns.

● 山西王家大院门帘架

门帘架上的三阳开泰图案周围点缀有花草，使图案更加丰富。刻出羊下巴上的胡子，使羊的形象更加生动，正中刻有太阳图案，松树寓意长寿。

Door Curtain Frame at Wang's Compound in Shanxi Province

The pattern of Three *Yang* Bringing out the Bliss on the door curtain frame is surrounded by floral decorations, making the overall pattern much more enriched. The beard on the chin of the goats (homonym to "*Yang*" in pronunciation) makes the goat images more vivid. In the center is a pattern of the sun. The pine trees symbolize longevity.

- **王家大院门帘架上雕刻的十鹿图**

在有限的框架里，把十头鹿的形象一一展现在画里，鹿奔跑、跳跃的姿态刻画逼真，对十头鹿不同方位的处理，使画面显得错落有致、疏密适宜。

10-deer Pattern Carved into the Door Curtain Frame at Wang's Compound

A picture of 10 deers is portrayed in the limited space of the framework, with each one of them realistically depicted in different postures of running and galloping. The handling of the directions of the 10 deers makes the picture look well-proportioned in the space with appropriate density.

> 罩

　　罩主要安装在室内柱间，用来分隔空间，集木雕、书法、绘画艺术等于一身，有很强的装饰功能。常见的有几腿罩、落地罩、栏杆罩、炕罩、圆光罩、八角罩等。罩多用硬木制作，雕工精细，纹饰美观。

> The Mask

The mask is mainly installed between indoor columns to separate the space. It comprises such elements as wood carving, calligraphy, artistic painting and so on and boasts strong decorative functions. Common masks include table-leg mask, down-to-ground mask, railing mask, the brick-bed mask, halo mask, octagonal mask and so forth. Masks are mostly made of hardwood with fine carvings and splendid decorations.

● **太极殿炕罩**

炕罩又叫床罩，是专门安放在床榻前面，用来遮挡床榻的，内侧可以悬挂幔帐和软帘。其形式与落地罩相同。室内顶棚过高时，可在炕罩上加顶盖，四周做毗卢帽、如意头等装饰。

Brick-bed Mask at the Taiji Hall

The brick-bed mask, also known as the bed mask, is specifically placed in front of the bed to mask the bed crouch. Curtains or soft drapes can be hung on the inside of it. It is in the same shape as the down-to-ground mask. If the ceiling of the room is too high, a cover may be added over the brick-bed mask, with monk-crown patterns, *Ruyi* head patterns or other ornaments on the four sides.

横披

horizontal hanging
scroll

槛框

railing frame

花罩或花牙子

floral mask (or
floral teeth)

- **长春宫栏杆罩**

栏杆罩由槛框、横披、花罩、栏杆等组成。栏杆罩有四根框落地，两根立框，两根抱框，划分出中间为主，两边为次的三开间形式。中间与几腿罩相同，但两边下安栏杆，故名。这种罩多用于进深较大的房间。

Railing Mask at the Palace of Eternal Spring

The railing mask is made up of the railing frame, the horizontal hanging scroll, the floral mask and the railing. A railing mask has four down-to-ground posts, namely, two standing posts and two holding posts, shaping up a three-width form with the central part as the primary body and both sides as the secondary. The central part looks like a table-leg mask with railings at the bottom of both sides, hence the name "railing mask". Railing masks are mostly used in rooms with greater depth.

- **安徽宏村承志堂几腿罩**

整组罩有两根腿子，腿子与上槛、挂空槛组成几案式框架，两根抱框恰似几腿，故名。适用于进深不大的房间。

Table-leg Mask at Chengzhi Hall in Hong Village, Anhui Province

The whole set of mask has two legs. Together with the upper rail and the hanging rail, they shape up a frame like one side of a tea table, hence the name "table-leg mask". It suits rooms of smaller depth.

- 北京北海静心斋落地罩

落地花罩形式与几腿罩相近，不同之处是横批下面的花罩沿两侧抱框向下延伸，到达地面，接须弥墩。这种罩的面积较大，装饰性很强。

Down-to-ground Mask in Jingxin Study at Beihai Park in Beijing

The down-to-ground mask looks very similar to table-leg mask in terms of pattern. The difference lies in the floral mask at the bottom of the horizontal hanging scroll, which crawls along the holding posts on both sides all the way down to the floor at the connection with the Buddhist Sumeru base. The down-to-ground mask is quite big and offers great decorative scope.

- 苏州耦园还研斋圆光罩

圆光罩、八角罩安装在室内进深柱间，做满装饰，中间留出圆形、八角形或其他形状的门洞，门洞内可以悬挂软帘，用来划分室内空间。

Halo Mask at the Huanyan Study in the Lotus Root Garden in Suzhou

The halo mask and octagonal mask are installed among pillars in rooms with depth to provide full-coverage decoration with a hole in the shape of a circle, an octagon or others, from which soft curtains can be hung for the purpose of separating the space inside the room.

＞天花

　　天花又称"顶棚"，是对室内顶部的装饰，不仅可以保暖、防尘等，还有很强的装饰作用。天花一般可分为硬天花、软天花。硬天花以木条纵横相交成若干格，每格上覆盖木板，称"天花板"，天

＞ The Ceiling Pattern

The ceiling pattern, or the plafond, refer to the decoration of the roof indoors. It does not only keep in the warmth, protect against dust but also has very powerful decorative effects. Generally, there are two types of ceilings, the hard one and the soft one. The hard ceiling is usually

● **团龙平棋**

由木肋格子和装填木板构成的大方格，犹如棋盘，因此称为"平棋天花"。格子上有彩绘或者雕花作为装饰。

Dragon Chessboard

The big square pattern composed of wood grids and covering boards bears a resemblance to a chessboard, which gives it the title of "chessboard ceiling". The grids are decorated with colored paintings or carvings.

- 海墁天花

海墁天花表面平坦，没有肋条，用木板做成，或是在较小的房间内架起一个完整的框架，上面安装木平板或糊纸，顶部彩绘成一整片。

Haiman Ceiling Patterns

The surface of the *Haiman* ceiling patterns is flat with no ribs. It is made of a wood board or a complete piece of frame, in the case of a smaller room, installed with a flat wood panel or pasted paper on it with the whole surface colorfully painted.

- 太和门团龙纹井口天花

由井字形木肋格子组成的天花，是天花的最高型制，清代时多用于宫殿建筑。

Compartment Ceiling with Coiled Dragon Patterns at the Gate of the Supreme Harmony

The ceiling pattern is composed of grids made of wood ribs in the shape of the Chinese character "井" (well). It is the highest form of ceiling patterns, mostly used in imperial palaces in the Qing Dynasty (1644-1911).

花板圆光中心常绘有龙、凤、吉祥花卉等图案。软天花又称"海墁天花"，以木格篦为骨架，满糊麻布和纸，上绘彩画或用编织物装饰。

structured into grids by wood strips vertically and horizontally intersected with one another. Each grid is covered with a board called ceiling board. The central halo of the ceiling board is usually painted with patterns of dragons, phoenixes, and auspicious flowers, etc. The soft ceiling, also called "ocean-covered ceiling", is made of wood castor-oil plant as the frame, pasted with sackcloth and paper with painted patterns or basketwork.

> 藻井

藻井是传统建筑的室内顶棚的独特装饰部分。"藻"即水藻，代表水；"井"为天文上所称的"东井"，为贮水之所，因此藻井有克火的含义，同时其又是传统建筑等级的一种体现。藻井用于宫殿宝座和寺庙神佛龛位的上空屋顶，南方

> The Caisson

The caisson (*Zao Jing* in Chinese) is the unique decorative part of the indoor ceiling in traditional architecture. "*Zao*" means algae, which stands for water; "*Jing*" refers to the Chinese astronomic terms of "east well", a place to store water. Therefore, caisson takes on the meaning of "subduing fire", and

- 四方形藻井
四方形藻井，又称"斗四藻井"，表面呈四方形，较为常见。
Square Caisson
Square caisson, also know as "Dou Si Caisson",is mostly seen with squares on the surface.

- 圆形藻井
福建泉州天后宫进门处戏台的圆形藻井，穹隆状，状似斗。
Round Caisson
Round caisson of the theater stage at the entrance of the Palace of the Queen of Heaven in Quanzhou, Fujian Province, takes the form of a dome like a funnel.

● 北京故宫澄瑞亭的八角藻井
Octagonal Caisson of the Pavilion of Pure Felicity in the Forbidden City, Beijing

祠堂、戏台中也使用藻井。藻井呈穹隆状，大多是用斗拱层层相叠而成，简单的藻井则用木板制作。藻井的形制有四方形、圆形和八角形等，也有将几种形状融为一体的，层层叠落，精美华丽。

embodies the ranks in traditional architectures. Caisson is used in the dome over the throne in the palace or over the shrine in the temple. In south China, it is also used in ancestral shrines or theaters. A caisson takes the shape of a dome. It is based on wood brackets put together layer by layer. The simple version of caisson used wood boards in its construction. There are square caissons, round ones, octagonal ones and so on. In some cases, a combination of several different types can be seen in layered cascades of great delicacy and splendor.

太和殿的盘龙藻井

北京故宫太和殿金銮宝座正上方的天花板上有一个盘龙藻井。此藻井分上、中、下三层，上圆下方，以斗拱承托，通高1.8 米，井口直径达6 米，顶部中央为圆形盖板，周围施以28 攒组成的小斗拱。穹隆圆顶心的明镜下盘卧着一条巨龙，口衔宝珠，俯首下视。龙口所衔的宝珠，名"轩辕镜"，为青铜制成，外涂水银，光亮如镜。在宝座的正上方悬轩辕镜，表示皇帝得位于大统，另一方面又寓指有雷雨之神坐镇于此，可保大殿安全。

Caisson with Coiled Dragons in the Hall of the Supreme Harmony

Over the golden throne in the Hall of the Supreme Harmony inside the Forbidden City in Beijing is a caisson with patterns of coiled dragons. It has upper, middle and lower layers, with the upper layer being round and the lower one square. Each layer is supported by brackets and tapers to the top with a vertical height of 1.8 meters and a diameter of as wide as 6 meters. In the center of the top is the round cover board, surrounded by 28 sets of small brackets. Under the clear mirror in the middle of the top dome lies a giant coiled dragon with a pearl in its mouth, looking downward. The pearl, called "*Xuan Yuan* mirror", is made of bronze, coated with mercury, making it as bright as a mirror. It is hung directly over the throne to indicate that the emperor is enthroned by the great unity. It also implies that the god of thunder and rain reside here to safeguard the hall.

● 太和殿盘龙藻井

顶部绘有或雕刻有盘龙纹的藻井，是最高等级的藻井，仅用于与皇帝有关的宫殿和最高等级的礼制坛庙。

Caisson with Coiled Dragons in the Hall of the Supreme Harmony

The top of the caisson is painted or carved with the pattern of coiled dragons. It is the highest-class caisson, used only in the emperor's palaces or the temples or shrines of the highest level in accordance with the ritual system.

> 碧纱橱

碧纱橱又作"壁纱橱"，是一种做工精细、通透的隔扇，由槛框、横披、隔扇等部分组成，安装在室内进深的柱间。碧纱橱视房间的大小，由6扇至12扇隔扇组成，其中只有两扇是活动扇，作为进出口。碧纱橱用料讲究，其上有精细的雕刻，上层的仔屉内有各种形式的棂条花纹。仔屉采用夹堂做法，屉有二层，中间夹入纱或玻璃，上面绘有花草鱼虫、人物故事，或题有诗词格言，具有很高的观赏价值。

> The Green Gauze Cabinet

The green gauze cabinet, or "wall gauze cabinet", is a fine work of transparent partition door made up of the frame, the horizontal hanging scroll and the partition door, installed between pillars in a room with ample depth. By size of the room, the green gauze cabinet may be composed of 6 to 12 partition doors, only two of which are movable to gain entry. The green gauze cabinet lays much stress on the selection of the materials, for intricate carvings are made on it. In the lattice on the upper part of it are various forms of lattice strips and floral patterns. The lattice is built of clipped frames in two layers with gauze or glass inserted in between. Patterns of flowers, grass, fish and insects, story pictures, or inscriptions of poems or maxims are painted on it, endowing it with a high value of appreciation.

隔扇
the partition door

槛框
the frame

横披
the horizontal hanging scroll

- 碧纱橱
  Green Gauze Cabinet

> 太师壁

太师壁是指明堂后檐金柱间的壁面装饰,多见于南方园林厅堂之中。壁前放置条几案等家具及各种陈设。太师壁从地面开始,高至屋梁,左右两侧留有空间供人通行。壁面有多种样式,有的以雕刻为主,有的是由隔扇组合而成,有的用棂条槛窗形式,有的则是在板壁上刻字挂画。

> The *Taishi* Wall

The *Taishi* wall is a wall decoration installed between the hypostyle columns of the back eave behind the main hall. It is often seen in the halls in gardens in south China. In front of it is put such furniture as long tables and various furnishings. The *Taishi* wall starts from the floor and rises up to the beam of the house with reserved space on its both sides to allow passage. The surface of the wall is variously featured, sometimes with carvings and other times with combined partition doors or grid-patterned windows. It may also take the shape of either the window frame with lattice bars or a board wall with carved texts or hung scrolls.

• 安徽程大位故居维新堂太师壁
Taishi Wall at Weixin Hall of Cheng Dawei's Former Residence in Anhui Province

> 博古架

博古架是用来陈设各种古玩的木架子。明清时期装饰室内时，在柱间设置不可移动的博古架，具有隔断和陈设家具的用途。一般分为上下两段，上段为博古架，分出许多形状不同的空格，空格中可陈列各种古玩，极其雅致。下段是有柜门的小柜橱，用来储藏古玩器具。由博古架分隔开的两个空间需要联通时，还可在博古架的中间或两侧留出通道，供人通行。其花格通透，将陈列的古玩衬托得富贵典雅。

> The Antique Shelf

The antique shelf (*Bogu Jia* in Chinese) is a wood shelf used to display various antiques. In the Ming and Qing Dynasties (1368-1911), the antique shelf was usually set immovably between pillars as interior decoration in order to separate the space and display articles. The shelf can be divided into two sections: the upper section is the antique shelf with spaces of different shapes to display various antiques in a very elegant way; the lower section is the small cabinet with doors to store antique articles. Sometimes, a passage may be spared in the middle or either side of the antique shelf to allow people to pass through between the spaces it divides. The open-space shelf serves well in striking a rich and elegant note in its exhibition of antiques.

博古架上部的花鸟图案，栩栩如生

vivid patterns of flowers and birds shown in
the upper part of the antique shelf

博古架顶部的龙形木雕

woodcarving in the shape of a dragon at
the top of the antique shelf

博古架腿足的植物纹样，精致细微

exquisite patterns of vegetation shown on
the foot of the antique shelf

● 博古架

Antique Shelf

博古

所有吉祥器物统称博古。建筑上雕刻的暗八仙、如意、贡果、花瓶、琴棋书画等具有吉祥寓意的纹饰都可以叫做博古纹，它是北宋以后中国古代常用的装饰性纹样。以这类题材作为装饰，寓意高洁、清雅。

Bogu

All auspicious objects are collectively referred to as *Bogu*. In architecture, any carvings with such auspicious items as an implied eight immortals pattern, *Ruyi*, tribute fruit, vases, and the combination of zither, chess, calligraphy and painting and so on are called the pattern of *Bogu*. The pattern of *Bogu* has been massively used as decorative patterns since the Northern Song Dynasty (960-1127). As a decorative theme, the pattern imparts a sense of nobility and elegance.

• 家具上的博古纹
Bogu of Furniture

《中国红》出版编辑委员会

主 任 王亚非

副 主 任 田海明 林清发

编 委 （以姓氏笔划为序）

      王亚非 毛白鸽 田海明 包云鸠

      孙建君 任耕耘 吕 军 吕品田

      吴 鹏 杜国新 林清发 赵国华

      徐 雯 涂卫中 唐元明 韩 进

      蒋一谈

执行编委 任耕耘 蒋一谈

传统手工艺
Traditional Chinese Crafts

风筝
Kites

面具
Masks

中国色彩
Colorful China

盆景
Bonsai

鼻烟壶
Snuff Bottles

刺绣
Chinese Embroidery

景泰蓝
Cloisonné

四大发明
Four Great Inventions of Ancient China

中国禅
Zen

泥塑
Clay Sculpture

丝绸之路
The Silk Road

棋艺
Art of Chesses

面塑
Dough Figuring

汉字
Chinese Characters

宋词
Ci-Poems of the Song Dynasty

大运河
Grand Canal

中国木偶艺术
Chinese Puppet Arts

茶马古道
Ancient Tea-Horse Road

中国历史名城
Historical Cities

古代兵书
Ancient Book on the Art of War

中国名湖
Famous Lakes in China

中国结
Chinese Knots

道教文化
Daoism Culture in China

北京中轴线
The central axis in Beijing

兵马俑
Terracotta Army

古代交通
Ancient Traffic

帝王陵寝
Imperial Mausoleum

皮影
Folk Shadow Play

古代壁画
Ancient Chinese Mural Painting

中华传统美德
Chinese Traditional Virtues

中国古代帝王
Emperors of China

古代衡器
Ancient Weighing Apparatus

中国姓氏
Chinese Surnames

中国陶器
Chinese Pottery Ware

24节气
The Twenty-four Solar Terms

传统家具
Chinese Furniture

中国漆器
Chinese Lacquer Articles

中国名泉
Famous Springs in China

中国名山
Renowned Chinese Mountains

中国名寺
Famous Temples in China

长江黄河
Yangtze River and Yellow River

中国染织
Chinese Dyeing and Weaving

中国石窟
Grottoes in China

传统杂技
Traditional Acrobatic Arts

武术
Chinese Martial Arts

中国古桥
Ancient Bridges in China

中国婚俗
Marriage Customs in China

民间玩具
Folk Toys

中国古塔
Ancient Pagodas in China

匾额对联
Inscribed Tablets and Couplets

古代教育
Education in Ancient China

中国民居
Traditional Civil Residents

中国建筑装饰
Chinese Architectural Decoration

中国神话传说
Chinese Mythology and Legends

民间戏曲
Traditional Folk Operas

十二生肖
The Twelve Animals Represent Years

古代游戏
Recreational Games in Ancient China

中国灯彩
Colorful Chinese Lanterns and Lamps

古代佩饰
Ornaments Wore by Ancient Chinese

四大名著
Four Masterpieces of Chinese Fiction

诸子百家
Traditional Philosophers and Ideologists

文房清供
Stationery and Bibelot in Ancient Studies

古代科技
Ancient China's Science and Technology

中国牌坊
Chinese Decorated and Memorial Archways

中国祥禽瑞兽
Auspicious Beasts and Fowls in Chinese Culture

金银器
Gold and Silver Wares

中国茶艺
Chinese Tea Appreciation Ceremony

竹木牙角器
Art Crafts Make of Bamboo, Wood, Ivory and Horn

秦砖汉瓦
Brick of Qin Dynasty and Tile of Han Dynasty